THE WOMAN'S DAY GREAT AMERICAN COOKIE BOOK

Edited by
JULIE HOUSTON

FAWCETT COLUMBINE • NEW YORK

THE WOMAN'S DAY GREAT AMERICAN COOKIE BOOK

Published by Fawcett Columbine Books, a unit of CBS Publications, the Consumer Publishing Division of CBS Inc.

Copyright © 1980 by CBS Publications, the Consumer Publishing Division of CBS Inc.

ALL RIGHTS RESERVED

ISBN: 0-449-90032-0

All photography by Ben Calvo, Woman's Day Studio

Printed in the United States of America

First Fawcett Columbine Printing: October 1980

10 9 8 7 6 5 4 3 2 1

CONTENTS

EDITOR'S INTRODUCTION

About Cookie Baking

Not long ago, in homes across the country, baking cookies was as much a part of the household routine as drying laundry outdoors in the fresh, clean air, keeping a stack of firewood outside the back door and setting a pie on the windowsill to cool.

No one thought twice about starting cookies from scratch or mixing them with loving care. All it took was a half-empty cookie jar, and out would come the wooden spoons and big ceramic mixing bowl. Soon the cookies would pop into the oven, and the kitchen would be filled with the warm, irresistible aroma of spices blending together in unmistakable combinations.

There were the everyday cookies—oatmeal and peanut butter, crisp molasses and chocolate chip—and then there were the special cookies. Greek almond *Kourabiedes*, Leckerli, Pfefferneusse and Hamantaschen—these were the ones that brought an extra measure of excitement to baking day, for they were reserved for festive occasions and holidays. Passed down from one generation to another, each recipe usually called for special ingredients and techniques, distinguishing the family's special heritage—and offering a vivid taste of the homeland.

In those days, everyone helped out, baking *and* tasting. Many a small hand eagerly licked the bowl and, too, many a small hand mischievously reached into the cookie jar—always to find it filled.

Today, perhaps because households are smaller and there are fewer helping hands, or because it seems too time-consuming, baking cookies at home has become the exception rather than the rule.

If this is the case in your home, something wonderful is missing. For if cookie baking is old-fashioned—soothing the spirit and stirring up happy memories of bygone days—nothing about this gentle and delectable kitchen art is outdated.

No dessert is more economical, sensible, or nutritional than cookies. A little dough goes a long way: one cup can produce three or four dozen small cookies or a couple of dozen larger ones. And served along with coffee after dinner, a cookie or two is just as satisfying at the end of a meal as a slice of cake—and is hundreds of calories less. Weight watchers know all too well that to eliminate favorite foods is not the answer to losing pounds; the most effective diets are those which stress moderation. Thus anyone who craves sweets and desserts after a meal will find a few cookies the perfect, and totally satisfying, substitute for richer pastries and concoctions. Just try it!

As for being time-consuming, cookie baking is inherently a stop-and-start process—all the better to undertake in a busy household. Unlike most baking, with cookies it could not be easier to stop at one stage today and start at the next stage tomorrow—or next week. No harm done to the cookies, no matter how many interruptions.

With a roll of cookie dough in the freezer, another batch chilled and ready to bake from the refrigerator and the cookie jar just filled, you'll suddenly find that homemade cookies are once again a part of the everyday routine!

About The Book

The pleasures of homemade cookies will come as no surprise to the readers of *Woman's Day*, nor will the appearance of this outstanding new book. Month after month, year after year, their favorite magazine has provided a steady offering of delectable cookie recipes—quick and easy bar cookies; big, plump drop cookies; crisp, lemony wafers; eye-pleasing pinwheels and crescents—each guaranteed to be tried-and-true favorites the first time out of the oven. Readers also found that they were getting an extra bonus by using the recipes from the magazine: long before the current nationwide focus on nutrition, *Woman's Day* recognized that cookies could provide far more than just munching, particularly among children just forming their eating habits. Every one of the dozen or so recipes that appear each month, whether an old standby or a totally new and delicious cookie, has been geared to satisfy a child's craving for sweets while providing an extra boost of nutrition.

Going back over twenty years of *Woman's Day* and considering literally thousands of cookie recipes for inclusion in this book, it quickly became apparent that the magazine's own high standards for every recipe would be the major challenge in making the final choice. *Every* recipe had something delectable going for it.

Narrowing down the recipes for the book became progressively more difficult. First it was a matter of ingredients—only the very best. Then it was a matter of selecting the best of those all-time unanimous favorites—fudgy chocolate brownies, chunky peanut-butter cookies, moist and chewy oatmeal cookies, for example—that kept appearing and reappearing over the years. Many, many variations appeared in this category alone, and it was important to select the freshest, most original recipes of all—the kind you really *would* want to repeat again and again.

From there, the goal was to broaden the base of the book: to choose as wide a sampling as possible of those other cookies which represent every facet and all the fun of baking cookies at home. Included are many recipes that are distinctly regional in character: Bourbon Brownies from the South, Harwich Hermits from New England, Pineapple Bars from the West Coast. There are others with the authentic flavors our forebears carried with them to this country: Edinburgh shortbread, French praline fingers and German Pfefferneusse, for example; still others with unexpectedly delicious and unusual combinations of ingredients, like Almond Oatmeal Cookies and Lemon Caraway Cookies. And then there are cookies with particularly intriguing textures and flavors due to their shaping and baking: Filbert Crescents, Jam Thimbles and Vanilla Pretzels, to name a few.

Finally, and unquestionably, the sum total of recipes here in *The Woman's Day Book of Great American Cookies* adds up to the best of the best: those recipes which, more than all the others, have a special way of making us feel that when the cookie jar is filled, it seems all's right with the world.

Julie D'Alton Houston,
Editor

I
THE COOKIE BAKER'S PANTRY

It's no wonder cookie baking fit so well into the family routine—all the basic ingredients are household staples and most of the other ingredients (those elements which distinguish one recipe from another) have a long shelf life.

So take inventory now and stock up on what is missing from the pantry. That way, next time the cookie jar is empty, it can be refilled with just about any of the delicious cookies in this book, without the need for a special shopping trip to buy ingredients. The list below should give you a head start.

Keep an eye out for specials in the supermarket, particularly on those ingredients that tend to be expensive—dried and candied fruits, canned nuts and chocolate. Sugar costs fluctuate dramatically, so stock up on and buy in quantity when prices are low.

Choose cookie recipes ahead of time and look them over now to see what can be done before baking day: dates, figs, prunes and nuts, for example, can all be chopped ahead of time.

Ingredients

FLOUR.
Buy large bags of white and whole-wheat flours. For extra nutrition, substitute a quarter cup of whole-wheat flour and three-quarters of a cup of white flour for every cup of white flour called for in bars and drop cookies.

SWEETENERS.
White sugar is a basic ingredient in most cookies, particularly in those simple recipes where the rich taste of butter stands out.

Light- or dark-brown sugar
is frequently used in spice cookies and many bars.

Confectioners' sugar
is used in frostings for bar cookies, and to coat many hand-shaped cookies.

Molasses
is a delicious sweetener in cookies, with a distinct flavor that dominates many of the very best old-fashioned cookies.

Honey

is called for in many recipes and can be used instead of, or in combination with, sugar in most drop cookies provided the cookies bake at temperatures no higher than 350°. If you are substituting honey for sugar, reduce the measurement by at least a few tablespoons since honey is much more concentrated a sweetener.

Note:

Cookies that contain high measures of honey, molasses or brown sugar tend to burn and should be watched as they bake.

SHORTENING.

There are purists, who will use only sweet butter in cookies, and there are pennypinchers, who will use only vegetable oils. Then there are the compromisers, who use a little of both in each recipe. With most cookies, the kind of shortening used is literally a matter of taste. Some cookies survive without butter; others lose that special something. In the long run, even if you hesitate to spend the money on real butter or to use it exclusively, it pays to add at least a few tablespoons of butter to the dough, as part of the shortening called for. Without exception, every cookie recipe will benefit from it in taste.

If you make this concession, buy sweet butter by the one-pound block, cut it into tablespoon-size bits and freeze it. That way, you need take out only what you need for the cookies and the butter will stay fresh.

SPICES. Cinnamon, cloves, nutmeg, ginger

—the standard spice rack usually contains all the basics for most cookies. For really first-rate flavor, grate your own nutmeg and fresh ginger. (The latter can be stored in the freezer.)

Cardamom,

with its very unusual taste, is used in many Scandinavian cookies, particularly around Christmastime.

Caraway seeds

also add a distinctive flavor, and are used in many recipes from Middle European countries.

DRIED FRUITS.

Usually the last ingredient to be mixed into the dough, dates, raisins, apricots, figs and other dried fruits add a flavor and texture that register immediately, with the first bite into a cookie. Naturally sweet, dried fruits are high in iron and extra nutritious when added to oatmeal and other drop cookies. When dried fruits are called for, try substituting one kind for another—currants or chopped prunes for raisins, for example, particularly when a substitute costs less. Chopped apricots in cookies are delicious.

COCONUT.
Raw coconut contains slightly more protein than canned, processed coconut and is much cheaper. Buy it shredded or grated, or grate your own and freeze it. It is also not sweetened, as processed coconut is.

NUTMEATS.
Keep a sealed can of nuts on the shelf: They are a standard ingredient in brownies and most bars and, whether called for or not, nuts are a delicious addition to almost any type of cookie. Packaged, whole pecans and almonds are more economical than canned ones, but time-consuming to prepare. The most economical way to buy nuts is to order them by mail directly from the orchards where they are grown.

CHOCOLATE.
Unsweetened squares are essential for brownies, just as real chocolate bits are for chocolate-chip cookies. Avoid premelted chocolate and artificial chocolate substitutes.

EGGS.
Use "Grade A Large," brought to room temperature.

PEANUT BUTTER.
Smooth or chunky, as is your fancy.

Jam,
for filled cookies. The classic filled cookie combination is raspberry-jam filling for butter cookies, but any good, thick jam will do, provided it is smooth in consistency. Prepare it ahead of time if necessary; force the jam through a sieve and store it in a jar in the refrigerator.

CANDIED FRUITS.
These are particularly popular for seasonal use, especially around Christmas.

PEARL SUGAR.
Some recipes call for pearl sugar, which is coarser than the granulated type. It can be found in specialty shops and in ethnic neighborhoods, particularly where middle-European families live. While it adds a distinctive texture, flavor will not be impaired if regular granulated or crushed lump sugar is used instead.

VANILLA
and other extracts. *Lemon* and *almond* are particular favorites for cookies.

Utensils

PANS.

Sizes most often used for bars and squares are at least 1½" high and measure 9" × 9", 9" × 13" or 9" × 12".

COOKIE SHEETS.

Use flat, low-rimmed aluminum sheets, allowing two inches of air space all around when placed in the oven. For assembly-line baking, it is practical to have two sheets on hand.

Note: Don't be lazy about a thorough clean-up of pans and sheets after the final baking. Every last trace of crumbs and grease should be removed—with an abrasive sponge, if necessary, and soap. Surfaces must be clean, smooth and nonsticky for successful cookie baking.

COOLING RACKS.

The mesh variety is best: the kind formed to stand up off the work surface by a few inches provides air circulation around the cookies as they cool. A good alternative is a barbeque rack placed over a bowl, right side up.

MEASURING EQUIPMENT.

Standard. For accuracy, hold spoons and cups at eye level when measuring.

MIXING BOWLS AND MIXING SPOONS.

A matter of personal choice. Like the carpenter who works best with his own familiar tools, many a cookie baker depends on a well-seasoned set of wooden mixing spoons and a heavy ceramic mixing bowl—held steady with one hand and a hip. Wooden spoons tend to pick up other kitchen odors (onions are notorious), so set aside a few spoons exclusively for mixing cookies.

A PASTRY CLOTH,

well floured, for rolling cookies will help avoid stickiness and overflouring of the dough.

A SOLID WOODEN ROLLING PIN

is the most efficient for rolling out cookie dough, but a glass bottle, although somewhat unwieldy, can be substituted.

COOKIE CUTTERS, PRESSES, MOLDS AND OTHER SPECIAL UTENSILS

are fun to collect even if they are used only once or twice a year around holidays or for special occasions. Rolled cookies can certainly be shaped and cut without them, however, so it's really a matter of sentiment—and kitchen storage space. Doughnut cutters are used frequently for filled cookies.

II
HOW TO BAKE GREAT COOKIES

This chapter contains everything a cookie baker needs to know, including all the little tips and hints from the magazine that make the difference between good cookies and great cookies.

It really doesn't take much to bake superb cookies. Mixing dough is easy, and with the right oven temperature and pans, all that is required is a careful eye to watch that they bake properly—not too long or too little—and that they're not too thick or too thin for the recipe used.

Baking

Use unsalted fats when greasing baking pans or cookie sheets. For drop cookies, there is no need to grease the entire sheet; just concentrate on the areas where the rows of cookies will go.

Preheat the oven and keep it at an even temperature throughout the baking.

Be energy conscious. Keep the top rack in your oven clear for a sheet of cookies, baked right along with today's main dish. Select cookie recipes in which dough can be prepared at least a day ahead or taken from the freezer and thawed in time for baking together with dinner.

If you are cooking several batches of cookies in one session, use no more than two sheets at a time in the oven.

Place the sheets at least two inches away from the sides of the oven. This allows air to circulate evenly around the cookies.

When baking several batches of cookies, be sure to bring the oven heat back up to the right temperature after opening and closing the doors. Since almost no home oven can be counted on to bake cookies evenly, be ready to turn the cookie sheets around if one end is browning faster than the other. Be particularly watchful with brown-sugar or molasses cookies, which tend to burn easily. You may have to take some of the cookies off the sheets and out of the oven if they appear to be done ahead of the others.

Assembly Lining

The "assembly-line" method of baking is an excellent way to cut down the time it takes to bake large batches of cookies. It really makes sense, particularly around the holidays.

The basic idea is to use the time while one batch of cookies is baking to prepare another batch for the oven.

Using two cookie sheets in the oven for each baking, you will need four pieces of foil. While one batch bakes (on two pieces of foil), get the other batch ready to bake (on the two remaining pieces of foil).

Transfer the foil off and onto the cookie sheets immediately after the cookies in the oven are done, but first run the cookie sheets under cool water to reduce heat.

Storing Cookies

You will soon find out that cookies seldom need special storage—they go too fast!

It is best to keep soft cookies in a sealed, airtight jar or tin container so they will not dry out. See-through plastic canisters are great for this purpose, but because the cookies are always in plain sight, they may prove too irresistible a temptation.

Old-fashioned decorative cookie jars (and there are many delightful reproductions on the market) are usually not airtight. Use them instead for crisp cookies, which are best stored in loosely sealed jars.

Be sure to store crisp varieties separately from soft ones. Otherwise, all the cookies will be soft in a day or so.

To keep soft cookies from getting dry, put a good, thick apple slice in the cookie jar and seal it up. This will also revive the original moist texture, if need be. Lemon or orange slices will bring the same results while adding extra zest.

If crisp cookies get soft, return them to a low oven for a few minutes to dry them out.

Freezing Cookies

To freeze baked cookies, wrap them tightly in aluminum foil. When you are ready to use them, thaw to room temperature (in single layers) and then pop them in a low (300° F.) oven for a few minutes to regain the original texture and flavor.

Before freezing cookie dough, which is possible with almost any such dough, first divide it into workable portions and then shape it for easy stacking in plastic bags in the freezer.

Keep a small plastic container in the freezer and add the crumbs from the cookie jar to it. A few heaping tablespoonsful can be used as topping for ice cream or puddings. (Heat up crumbs first to revive their flavor.) Or fold them into whipped cream for a delicious topping on fresh-fruit desserts.

Sending Cookies Through the Mail

This is a tradition in many families around the holidays, and a wonderful way to express love and affection at any time of year. Children away at camp or at college are especially cheered by this special treat.

Good sense should help you choose the best cookies to mail. Obviously, delicate wafers will end up as a box of crumbs no matter how carefully they were packed for shipping.

Look for recipes in the book that are earmarked for shipping, and choose similar types for variety. Many kinds of drop cookies are ideal candidates, and bar cookies are the best of all for mailing.

Use a strong box for mailing. Wrap cookies individually in wax paper or plastic wrap (no more than two cookies together, back to back), and separate each layer of cookies with a sheet of waxed paper or cardboard. Fill every space possible, and then pack the box in a carton, surrounded tightly with popcorn, styrofoam "bits" or plastic "bubble" sheeting. (The latter two are used commercially and are well worth saving or seeking out. Many appliance companies, camera manufacturers or bookstores throw the stuff out.)

Christmas Cookies

Everybody loves the idea of holiday baking, but it takes careful planning of time and a sensible choice of recipes to keep the holiday spirit a part of the baking. In most homes, there is no busier time of year than the Christmas holidays, and once cookie baking becomes a last-minute ordeal, even the most placid temperaments sizzle. So plan in advance. Choose recipes that can be prepared in stages, mix up quickly or freeze successfully. Choose a variety of cookies to bake, but balance the more time-consuming rolled and decorated cookies with easy refrigerator or bar cookies. Prepare several batches of cookie dough in early November and freeze them before the holiday momentum picks up. Or bake cookies just after Thanksgiving and freeze them until Christmas—it's a great way to launch the holiday season!

Thread Christmas-cookie tree ornaments before baking, pressing the thread into the dough, or make a neat hole in the dough with the point of a knife, for threading later.

Be sure to include children in the fun of baking Christmas cookies. Many hands *do* make light work, and there are many areas of baking that even the youngest members of the household can enjoy.

Bazaars

Because you can charge proportionately more for small units than you can for one large cake, homemade cookies, squares and bars are perfect for selling at bazaars and local fairs. Old-fashioned chocolate-chip cookies and rich brownies are perennial bestsellers, but there are dozens of recipes in this book for other cookies that will "go like hotcakes." Look for recipes that yield large quantities.

Wrap bars individually in see-through plastic and box them in reusable aluminum-foil pans (saved from frozen foods) for transporting and displaying.

Bag cookies in see-through plastic tied with ribbon, or sell them individually from clear plastic boxes. The kind of box sold for sweater storage is ideal for this purpose and can be used again and again, year after year.

When pricing the cookies, be sure to take into account the cost of all your ingredients and packing materials. Mark up accordingly, at least doubling your costs. You are guaranteed to make a nice profit for the group while offering a tasty bargain over store-bought baked goods.

Many recipes in this book can be doubled or even tripled for bazaar sales and other bake sales. Look for those that pack and transport well, will not break or lose flavor quickly.

Bar cookies are fastest to make when cooking in quantity, but for other types, the assembly-line method described earlier is ideal.

For novelty—and for more profit—bake cookies in giant sizes and sell them by the piece.

III
BARS AND SQUARES

From brownies to date bars to pecan squares, nothing could be easier or more delectable to bake at home than squares and bars.

As a group, bars and squares could be described as small cakes, but they share more of the versatility of cookies than do cakes.

Depending on the size of the pan, the same recipe will turn out chewy and moist bars or bars cakelike in texture. Generally, a smaller pan than called for will produce a more cakelike bar, but the kind of ingredients used will also influence texture. Dried fruits, candied fruits, flaked coconut, for example, will always keep bars and squares moist. And oatmeal or large quantities of brown sugar will always keep them chewy. Plain, smooth batters tend to produce bars cakelike and more delicate in flavor than those calling for many ingredients.

Whichever your preference, the dough for squares and bars should be spread out in the pan to no less than one and a half inches in thickness. Obviously, if you use a different pan size than is specified in a recipe, adjust the baking time to more for a smaller pan, less for a larger one. You must be the judge of when the bars are ready. Watch the bars closely as they bake—they are done when a pick inserted in the center comes out clean. In any case, most bars bake successfully at between 325° and 350°. Thus they are perfectly suited to "sharing" the oven with a main-dish casserole or roast, thereby saving energy.

Take care to keep bars from sticking by greasing and then flouring pans. Plain bread crumbs can be substituted for flour.

When squares and bars are baked to "travel," whether to a picnic next door or to a friend across the country, wrap them individually in cellophane or waxed paper. This gives them an especially neat appearance.

For the most appealing presentation, always cut squares and bars into clean, uniform pieces—after the pan has cooled down and the bars "set." The richer the bar, the smaller the piece.

To give them a distinctive taste, top squares and bars with your own favorite frostings and sweet glazes.

Brownies and Other Chocolate Bars

SUPERFUDGY SAUCEPAN BROWNIES
(shown on plate 3)

The easiest kind of all, mixed in the saucepan used to melt the chocolate. Use 6 squares chocolate for extra–superfudgy brownies.

1 cup flour	⅔ cup butter or
1 teaspoon each	margarine
baking powder and	2 cups sugar
salt	4 eggs
4 to 6 squares (4 to 6	2 teaspoons vanilla
ounces)	1½ cups chopped
unsweetened	nuts
chocolate	

Mix well flour, baking powder and salt; set aside. In large saucepan melt chocolate and butter over low heat. Stir in sugar, eggs, vanilla and flour mixture, then nuts. Turn into greased 13 × 9 × 2-inch pan. Bake in preheated 350° F. oven 25 minutes or until finger pressed lightly on surface leaves slight indentation. Cool in pan on rack. Cut in 48 bars. **NOTE:** Recipe can be halved and baked in 8 × 8 × 2-inch pan.

CHOCOLATE BROWNIES

An excellent recipe for quantity cooking.

12 squares (12	6 cups sugar
ounces)	4 teaspoons vanilla
unsweetened	1 teaspoon salt
chocolate	3¼ cups all-purpose
1 pound butter or	flour
margarine	5 cups chopped
1 dozen eggs	walnuts or pecans

Melt chocolate and butter together in heavy saucepan. Beat eggs until thick. Gradually beat in sugar, then beat in chocolate mixture. Add vanilla, salt and flour and mix well. Fold in nuts. Spread in 3 greased 15 × 10 × 1-inch pans and bake in preheated 325°F. oven 25 to 30 minutes. Cool in pans, then cut each in 35 pieces.

MARBLE BROWNIES

These rich, moist brownies are a chocolate fiend's delight.

1 cup butter or
  margarine, softened
1½ teaspoons vanilla
2 cups sugar
4 eggs
1¾ cups flour
½ teaspoon salt

2 cups coarsely
  chopped nuts
2 squares (2 ounces)
  unsweetened
  chocolate, melted
  and cooled
Velvety Chocolate
  Frosting (recipe
  follows)

Cream butter, vanilla and sugar until light and fluffy. Add eggs one at a time, beating well after each. Add flour and salt and mix until blended. Stir in nuts. Divide batter in half and add chocolate to half. Drop batters alternately by heaping teaspoonfuls into greased 13 × 9 × 2-inch pan lined on bottom with waxed paper. Press with spoon to smooth top and run knife through batter several times to marbleize. Bake in preheated 350°F. oven about 45 minutes. Turn out on cake rack and peel off paper at once. Cool and frost. At serving time cut in about 24 squares.

Velvety Chocolate Frosting

¼ cup hot water
2¼ cups
  confectioners'
  sugar
4 squares (4 ounces)
  unsweetened
  chocolate, melted

4 egg yolks
¼ cup butter or
  margarine, melted
1 teaspoon vanilla

Add hot water and sugar to chocolate and mix well. Add egg yolks one at a time, beating well after each. Slowly add butter, then vanilla and beat until smooth. If too thin to spread immediately, let stand a few minutes to thicken. Makes enough for 13 × 9-inch rectangle or two 8-inch cake layers.

CHOCOLATE-CINNAMON BROWNIES

1 cup flour	2 squares (2 ounces)
1 teaspoon cinnamon	unsweetened
½ teaspoon each	chocolate
baking powder and	1 cup sugar
salt	2 eggs
½ cup butter or	1 teaspoon vanilla
margarine	1 cup chopped nuts

Stir together flour, cinnamon, baking powder and salt; set aside. Melt butter and chocolate in heavy saucepan over low heat. Meanwhile beat sugar, eggs and vanilla until thick and lemon-colored; add flour and chocolate mixtures, beating with spoon until smooth. Stir in nuts, then spread in greased 9-inch square pan. Bake in preheated 350°F. oven about 30 minutes. Cool in pan on rack. Cut in 16 brownies about 2 inches square.

BOURBON BROWNIES

A Southern treat.

⅓ cup margarine or	¾ cup all-purpose
butter	flour
2 squares (2 ounces)	¼ teaspoon salt
unsweetened	3 tablespoons (about)
chocolate	bourbon
½ teaspoon vanilla	Tinted almonds or
1 cup sugar	granulated sugar
2 eggs	

Melt margarine and chocolate in saucepan over low heat, stirring; cool. Beat in vanilla and sugar. Add eggs one at a time, beating well after each. Mix flour and salt and stir into chocolate mixture. Spread in greased 8-inch square pan. Bake in slow oven (325°F.) about 25 minutes; cool. When thoroughly cooled, crumble brownies into bowl. Sprinkle with bourbon; mix in with fingers. Shape in 1-inch balls or logs about 1-inch long. Roll in Tinted Almonds. Store in airtight container for a day before serving or giving. To give, put in metal star mold and cover with foil. Trim with greens and ornament. Makes 3 to 3½ dozen.

CHOCOLATE-WALNUT SQUARES

A rich, candylike confection.

½ cup butter or
  margarine
¾ cup sifted
  confectioners'
  sugar
4 eggs, separated
3 squares (3 ounces)
  semisweet
  chocolate, melted
  and cooled

1 cup walnuts,
  ground
2 tablespoons flour
½ teaspoon vanilla
Walnut Filling
Chocolate Glaze
25 walnut halves

Cream butter until very light. Add sugar a little at a time, beating well after each addition. Beat egg yolks until light and lemon-colored, then beat into butter mixture. Add next 4 ingredients and mix well. Beat egg whites until stiff and fold gently into batter. Turn into 2 well-greased 8-inch square pans. Bake in preheated 350°F. oven about 20 minutes. Cool a few minutes, then turn out on cake rack. When cool, prepare filling and spread between layers. Cut in 1½-inch squares. Spread top and sides with glaze and top each square with a walnut half before glaze sets. Makes 25.

Walnut Filling

1 square (1 ounce)
  semisweet
  chocolate
3 tablespoons sugar
1 cup walnuts, ground

¼ cup milk
2 tablespoons butter
  or margarine
½ teaspoon vanilla

Melt chocolate in top of double boiler over hot, not boiling, water. Add sugar, walnuts and milk and cook, stirring, until thickened. Remove from heat. Add butter and vanilla and beat until thoroughly cooled.

Chocolate Glaze

1 package (6 ounces)
  semisweet
  chocolate pieces
2 tablespoons butter
  or margarine

2 tablespoons light
  corn syrup
3 tablespoons milk

Melt chocolate and butter in top of double boiler over hot, not boiling, water. Stir in corn syrup and milk and beat until smooth.

GLAZED MINT-FROSTED BROWNIES

½ cup butter or margarine, softened	½ cup chopped nuts
1 cup sugar	½ cup flour
1 teaspoon vanilla	Mint Frosting
2 eggs	Chocolate Glaze
2 squares (2 ounces) unsweetened chocolate, melted and cooled	

In large bowl of mixer beat butter, sugar, vanilla, eggs and chocolate until well blended. Stir in nuts and flour. Spread in greased 8 × 8 × 2-inch baking pan. Bake in preheated 350°F. oven 25 minutes or until top is firm. Cool, then spread with Mint Frosting. Let stand until set. Pour Chocolate Glaze over frosting and spread in thin, even layer. Chill until firm. Bring to room temperature before cutting. Makes about 24 bars.

MINT FROSTING Beat until smooth 1 cup confectioners' sugar, 2 tablespoons softened butter or margarine, 1 tablespoon milk and ½ teaspoon peppermint extract.

CHOCOLATE GLAZE In small saucepan over low heat melt 2 tablespoons butter or margarine. Add 2 squares (2 ounces) unsweetened chocolate and stir to melt and until smooth.

COCOA-GRAHAM BARS

(shown on plate 3)

2 cups graham-cracker crumbs	1 teaspoon vanilla
⅓ cup cocoa	Confectioners' sugar
1 can (14 ounces) sweetened condensed milk	

Mix well crumbs and cocoa. Blend in milk and vanilla. Spread evenly in greased 8 × 8 × 2-inch pan. Bake in preheated 350°F. oven 25 minutes or until pick inserted in center comes out clean. Cool in pan on rack. Cut in 24 bars, then sprinkle with confectioners' sugar.

FUDGY OATMEAL SQUARES
(shown on plate 8)

1 cup instant rolled oats	1 teaspoon baking soda
1½ cups boiling water	½ teaspoon salt
1 cup flour	½ cup shortening
1½ cups granulated sugar	1 teaspoon vanilla
½ cup cocoa	2 eggs
	Confectioners' sugar (optional)

Stir together oats and water; set aside. In large bowl of mixer stir together flour, granulated sugar, cocoa, soda and salt. Add shortening, oat mixture and vanilla; beat at low speed just until mixed, then beat at medium speed 2 minutes, scraping bowl frequently. Add eggs; beat at medium speed 2 minutes, scraping bowl occasionally. Pour into greased 13 × 9 × 2-inch pan. Bake in preheated 350°F. oven 35 minutes or until pick inserted in center comes out clean. Cool in pan 10 minutes, then turn out on rack and cool completely. Sprinkle with confectioners' sugar. Cut in squares. Makes about 24.

THIN CHOCOLATE BROWNIE BARS

A crisp, chewy cookie that keeps well.

1 square (1 ounce) unsweetened chocolate	¼ cup flour
¼ cup butter or margarine	1 teaspoon vanilla
½ cup sugar	⅛ teaspoon salt
1 egg	⅓ cup chopped walnuts, pecans or filberts

Melt chocolate and butter in heavy saucepan over low heat (mixture should be melted but not hot). Remove from heat; stir in sugar. Add egg, flour, vanilla and salt; mix well. Spread evenly in greased 13 × 9 × 2-inch pan and sprinkle with walnuts. Bake in preheated 400°F. oven 12 minutes or until top is firm to touch. Cool slightly; cut in bars (must be cut while hot). When cool, remove from pan to racks to crisp. Makes 24 to 30.

CHOCOLATE BUTTERSCOTCH BARS

They have walnuts in them, too.

⅔ cup shortening, melted
2¼ cups light-brown sugar, packed
3 eggs
2¾ cups sifted flour
½ teaspoon salt

2½ teaspoons baking powder
1 cup chopped California walnuts
1 package (6 ounces) semisweet chocolate pieces
1 teaspoon vanilla

Add shortening to sugar and mix well. Add eggs, one at a time, beating thoroughly after each. Add sifted dry ingredients, nuts, chocolate and vanilla. Spread in greased 15 × 10 × 1-inch pan. Bake in moderate oven (350°F.) about 25 minutes. While warm, cut in 50 bars.

MOCHA BARS

1 cup butter or margarine, softened
1 cup packed brown sugar
2¼ cups flour
1 teaspoon dry instant coffee
½ teaspoon baking powder

¼ teaspoon salt
1 teaspoon almond extract
1 package (6 ounces) semisweet chocolate pieces
½ cup chopped almonds

In large bowl of electric mixer, cream butter and sugar until fluffy. Stir together flour, coffee, baking powder and salt; beat well into creamed mixture. Stir in extract, chocolate and almonds. Press dough in greased 15 × 10 × 1-inch pan and bake in preheated 350°F. oven about 25 minutes. Cut in bars while warm. Makes about 5 dozen cookies.

CHOCOLATE SHORTBREAD

A chocolate lover's treat from Scotland.

1 cup butter, softened
1 cup sugar

2½ cups all-purpose
flour
⅓ cup sifted
unsweetened cocoa

Cream together butter and sugar until light and fluffy. Sift flour and cocoa into creamed mixture and stir in thoroughly. Divide dough in half. Press each half evenly on bottom of a 9-inch pie pan, pinching edge to form a fluted rim. Prick all over with a fork. Mark each pan in 16 wedges, cutting about halfway through dough. Bake in slow oven (300°F.) 35 to 40 minutes, or until firm when pressed gently in center. Cut through marks. Cool in pans on racks. Makes 32 pieces.

CHOCOLATE-CHIP COCONUT BARS
(shown on plate 2)

2 eggs
¾ cup packed light-
brown sugar
½ cup flour
¼ teaspoon each salt
and baking soda

1 teaspoon vanilla
1 cup shredded or
flaked coconut
½ cup semisweet
chocolate pieces

Beat eggs and sugar until smooth. Beat in flour, salt, soda, vanilla and coconut. Turn into greased 8 × 8 × 2-inch pan. Sprinkle with chocolate pieces. Bake in preheated 350°F. oven 25 minutes or until pick inserted in center comes out clean. Cool completely in pan on rack. Cut in 18 bars.

Fruit Bars

APPLESAUCE BARS

2 cups all-purpose
  flour
1 teaspoon baking
  soda
¾ teaspoon cinnamon
¼ teaspoon nutmeg
½ cup butter or
  margarine, softened
1 cup granulated
  sugar

2 eggs
1 teaspoon vanilla
1½ cups applesauce
1 cup chopped
  walnuts or pecans
1 cup raisins
Confectioners' sugar

Mix flour with soda and spices. Cream butter with granulated sugar until light and fluffy. Add eggs and vanilla and beat well. Stir in flour mixture. Add applesauce, nuts and raisins and stir until blended. Pour into greased 15 × 10 × 1-inch pan. Bake in preheated 350°F. oven 25 minutes, or until done. Cool, then cut in 2½- × 1-inch bars and sprinkle with confectioners' sugar. Makes 56 bars.

APRICOT SQUARES

Fresh, fragrant and delicious.

½ cup butter or
  margarine, softened
1½ cups packed
  brown sugar,
  divided
1¼ cups plus 3
  tablespoons flour
2 eggs
1 cup finely chopped
  or snipped dried

apricots (about 6
  ounces)
¾ cup flaked coconut
½ cup chopped
  pecans
½ teaspoon vanilla
½ teaspoon lemon
  juice
¼ teaspoon salt

Mix well butter, ½ cup brown sugar and 1¼ cups flour. Press into ungreased 13 × 9 × 2-inch baking pan. Bake in preheated 350°F. oven 10 minutes. Meanwhile blend remaining 1 cup sugar, eggs, apricots, coconut, pecans, remaining 3 tablespoons flour, vanilla, lemon juice and salt. Spread over baked crust. Bake 25 minutes or until pick inserted in center comes out clean. Cool and cut in 32 squares. Will keep in airtight container in cool place about 2 weeks.

DUNDEE TEA BARS

A festive fruitcake bar, topped with a lemon glaze.

½ cup soft butter or
  margarine
½ cup sugar
1 teaspoon vanilla
2 eggs
1½ cups sifted flour
1 teaspoon baking
  powder
¼ teaspoon salt

½ teaspoon nutmeg
¼ cup chopped
  candied cherries
¼ cup chopped
  candied pineapple
¼ cup chopped citron
¼ cup raisins
Lemon Glaze

Cream butter and sugar until light. Beat in vanilla and eggs. Add sifted dry ingredients and fruit; mix well. Pour into a 9-inch-square pan, lined on the bottom with waxed paper. Bake in moderate oven (325°F.) 25 to 30 minutes. Turn out on rack and peel off paper. Turn right side up and brush with glaze. Cool and cut in 24 bars. (Good keepers and shippers.)

GLAZE: Mix ¼ cup sifted confectioners' sugar, 1 teaspoon water and ½ teaspoon lemon juice.

NOTE: ¾ cup candied mixed fruit can be substituted for the cherries, pineapple and citron.

FESTIVE RAISIN SQUARES

The pungent flavor of ginger blends perfectly with raisins, nuts and coconut.

½ cup butter or
  margarine, softened
1¼ cups packed
  brown sugar
½ teaspoon salt
All-purpose flour
2 eggs
1 teaspoon vanilla

½ teaspoon baking powder
1 cup chopped
  seedless raisins
¾ cup flaked coconut
¾ cup chopped
  pecans or other nuts
2 tablespoons minced
  candied ginger

Cream butter with ¼ cup sugar and ¼ teaspoon salt until fluffy. Mix in 1 cup flour. Spread in 8-inch square pan and bake in slow oven (325°F.) 15 minutes, or until golden brown. Beat eggs until light and fluffy. Beat in remaining sugar and the vanilla. Add remaining salt, 2 tablespoons flour and the baking powder. Mix well and add remaining ingredients. Carefully spoon onto baked crust and bake 35 minutes longer, or until firm. Cool and cut in 16 squares.

COCONUT ORANGE SQUARES

Easy to make because they mix quickly.

¼ cup soft butter or
    margarine
1 cup sugar
1 egg
1 tablespoon grated
    orange rind

1 tablespoon milk
1 cup flaked coconut
⅔ cup sifted flour
½ teaspoon baking
    powder
½ teaspoon salt

Cream butter and sugar until light. Beat in egg, orange rind and milk. Add coconut, and flour sifted with baking powder and salt. Mix only enough to blend. Put in 8-inch-square pan, lined with waxed paper. Bake in moderate oven (350°F.) about 25 minutes. Cut in 16 squares.

CHEWY COCONUT SQUARES
(shown on plate 2)

¼ cup butter or
    margarine, softened
¾ cup sugar, divided
Flour
⅛ teaspoon salt

1 teaspoon vanilla
1 egg
½ cup chopped nuts
½ cup shredded or
    flaked coconut

Cream butter and ¼ cup sugar until light. Stir in ½ cup flour. Pat into greased 8 × 8 × 2-inch pan. Bake in preheated 350°F. oven 10 minutes. Meanwhile mix remaining ½ cup sugar, 2 tablespoons flour, the salt, vanilla, egg, nuts and coconut. Spread evenly over baked dough. Bake 25 minutes or until golden. While warm, cut in 25 squares. Cool in pan on rack.

DATE CHEWS
(shown on plate 3)

½ cup sugar
½ cup flour
½ teaspoon baking
    powder
⅛ teaspoon salt

1 cup chopped pitted
    dates
1 egg, beaten
Confectioners' sugar
    (optional)

Mix well sugar, flour, baking powder, salt and dates. Stir in egg until well mixed. (Dough will be very thick.) Spread evenly in greased 9 × 9 × 2-inch pan. Bake in preheated 350°F. oven 20 minutes or until rich golden, and pick inserted in center comes out clean. While warm, cut in 36 squares. Cool in pan on rack. Sprinkle with confectioners' sugar.

HARWICH HERMITS

Hermits, rich with spices, plump with fruits and nuts, originated in the seafaring town of Harwich on Cape Cod. Women made hermits for their menfolk to take on long voyages; they packed the hermits in tole canisters and tucked them away in sea chests.

½ cup butter or
  margarine
½ cup sugar
2 eggs, well beaten
½ cup molasses
2 cups all-purpose
  flour
½ teaspoon salt

1 teaspoon baking
  powder
1 teaspoon cinnamon
½ teaspoon ground
  cloves
¼ teaspoon mace
¼ teaspoon nutmeg
⅛ teaspoon allspice

3 tablespoons
  chopped citron
¼ cup raisins,
  chopped
½ cup currants,
  chopped
¼ cup nutmeats,
  broken

Cream butter and sugar until light. Add eggs and molasses. Beat well. Sift flour with salt, baking powder and spices. Stir fruits into ¼ cup flour mixture to keep from sticking together. Combine all ingredients and mix well. Spread evenly in buttered 13 × 9 × 3-inch pan. Bake in moderate oven (350°F.) 25 to 30 minutes, or until done. Cut into 24 bars while warm. Cool in pan, remove and store cookies in airtight container.

GINGER-PEAR BARS

You need fresh pears and crystallized ginger for the filling.

¾ cup soft butter or
  margarine
1 cup packed light-
  brown sugar
2 cups unsifted all-
  purpose flour
1 teaspoon salt

½ teaspoon baking
  soda
½ cup finely chopped
  nuts
1½ cups flaked
  coconut
Ginger-Pear Filling

Cream butter and sugar until light and fluffy. Add sifted dry ingredients, nuts and coconut and mix well. Press three-fourths of mixture into lightly greased 9-inch square pan. Cover with filling. Sprinkle remaining mixture over top. Bake in moderate oven (350°F.) 35 to 40 minutes. Cool and cut in bars about 2 inches × 1 inch. Makes 36.

GINGER-PEAR FILLING Force enough peeled fresh pears through food chopper to make 1 cup. Put in saucepan and add 1½ teaspoons cornstarch, ½ cup sugar and 1 tablespoon chopped crystallized ginger. Bring to boil and simmer 20 minutes, stirring frequently. Add ½ teaspoon grated lemon rind and 1½ teaspoons lemon juice. Cool to room temperature.

PRUNE HERMIT BARS

(shown on plate 2)

1 cup flour
1 teaspoon baking
    powder
½ teaspoon cinnamon
¼ teaspoon cloves
⅛ teaspoon baking
    soda
⅛ teaspoon salt
¼ cup butter or
    margarine, softened

¼ cup sugar
1 egg
¼ cup molasses
½ cup snipped prunes
½ cup chopped nuts
Lemon-Cheese
    Frosting (recipe
    follows)
24 nut halves
    (optional)

Mix well flour, baking powder, cinnamon, cloves, baking soda and salt; set aside. In large bowl cream butter and sugar until light. Beat in egg, then molasses, until well blended. Stir in flour mixture, prunes and chopped nuts until well mixed. Turn into greased 9 × 9 × 2-inch pan. Bake in preheated 350°F. oven 25 to 30 minutes or until pick inserted in center comes out clean. Cool in pan on rack. Spread evenly with frosting. Cut in 24 bars. Garnish each with nut half.

LEMON-CHEESE FROSTING In bowl mix well 4 ounces (half 8-ounce package) softened cream cheese, 2 tablespoons sugar, 1 tablespoon milk and 2 teaspoons grated lemon peel.

LEMON-CURRANT SQUARES

Delectably rich. The currants keep them moist.

1 cup butter or
    margarine, softened
1 cup sugar
1 egg, beaten
1 teaspoon vanilla
2 cups flour

1 teaspoon grated
    lemon peel
1 cup dried currants,
    scalded and well
    drained
Confectioners' sugar

In large bowl of electric mixer cream butter and sugar until light and fluffy; beat in egg and vanilla; gradually beat in flour until well blended. With wooden spoon stir in peel and currants. Pour into greased, floured 13 × 9 × 2-inch pan and bake in preheated 325°F. oven 35 minutes. When cool, sprinkle generously with confectioners' sugar and cut in 24 squares.

LEMON SQUARES
(shown on plate 2)

1 cup shredded or flaked coconut	½ cup butter or margarine
Flour	2 eggs
Granulated sugar	¼ cup lemon juice
¼ teaspoon salt	Confectioners' sugar

Combine coconut, 1 cup flour, 2 tablespoons granulated sugar and the salt. Cut in butter until mixture is crumbly. Gather particles and with lightly floured fingertips press evenly and firmly over bottom and ¾ inch up sides of 9 × 9 × 2-inch baking pan. Bake in preheated 350°F. oven until golden, about 20 minutes. Meanwhile in small bowl beat together eggs, ¾ cup granulated sugar, 2 tablespoons flour and the lemon juice. Pour over crust and continue to bake until set, about 20 minutes. Cool in pan on rack. Cut in 16 squares, then sprinkle with confectioners' sugar.

PINEAPPLE BARS

2½ cups flour	1 egg, separated
⅓ cup sugar	⅔ cup pineapple preserves
¼ teaspoon salt	½ cup chopped nuts
1 cup butter or margarine	

In bowl combine flour, sugar and salt. Cut in butter until mixture resembles coarse crumbs. Stir in egg white and, with hand, gather in ball. Cut off a third, wrap and chill. Press remaining dough on bottom of 13 × 9 × 2-inch baking pan. Bake in preheated 375°F. oven until dry to touch, about 12 minutes. Cool in pan on rack. Spread with thin layer preserves. Sprinkle with nuts. On lightly floured surface roll out remaining chilled dough ⅛-inch thick. With pastry wheel or sharp knife cut ½-inch-wide strips. Arrange crisscross over preserves, leaving about ¾ inch between strips. (Pinch strips together if they break or are not long enough.) Brush strips with slightly beaten egg yolk. Bake 15 minutes or until golden brown. Cool on rack before cutting. Store airtight in cool, dry place. Makes about 32.

Nut Bars and Squares

SWEDISH NUT SQUARES
(Nötrutor)

A rich nut topping is spread over the dough before baking.

½ cup butter or
  margarine
¾ cup granulated
  sugar
2 eggs, beaten
2 cups all-purpose
  flour (instant type
  can be used)
1 teaspoon baking
  powder

½ teaspoon salt
2 tablespoons light
  cream
1½ teaspoons vanilla
2 egg whites, beaten
  stiff
1 cup packed brown
  sugar
1 cup chopped
  walnuts

Cream butter and granulated sugar. Add beaten eggs. Mix flour, baking powder and salt. Add alternately with cream to first mixture. Add 1 teaspoon vanilla. Spread in greased 15 × 10 × 1-inch pan. In heavy saucepan, mix egg whites, brown sugar and nuts. Heat gently 2 or 3 minutes, stirring. Add remaining vanilla and spread on dough. Bake in moderate oven (350°F.) about 25 minutes. Cool slightly and cut in squares. Makes about 4 dozen.

PECAN CRISPS

These delicious cookies are brittle, so save them for giving by hand.

1 cup soft butter
1 cup light-brown
  sugar, packed
1 teaspoon vanilla
1 egg, separated

2 cups sifted flour
½ teaspoon salt
1 teaspoon cinnamon
1 cup finely chopped
  pecans

Cream butter and sugar until light. Beat in vanilla and egg yolk. Add sifted dry ingredients and ½ cup of the nuts; mix well. Press into greased 15 × 10 × 1-inch pan and brush top with slightly beaten egg white. Sprinkle with ½ cup nuts. Bake in moderate oven (350°F.) about 25 minutes. While warm, cut in 50 bars. Remove at once to rack.

NUT SQUARES
(shown on plate 5)

Crunchy nut topping on a cookie crust.

½ cup butter or
   margarine, softened
½ cup packed brown
   sugar, divided
1 teaspoon vanilla
⅛ teaspoon salt
1 egg, separated

1¼ cups flour
1 cup finely chopped
   nuts
½ teaspoon cinnamon
Confectioners' sugar
   (optional)

In large bowl of mixer cream butter, ¼ cup brown sugar, vanilla and salt until fluffy. Add egg yolk and beat well. Stir in flour until blended. With floured fingertips press dough on bottom of lightly greased 8 × 8 × 2-inch baking pan. Bake on lowest rack in preheated 350°F. oven 10 minutes. Meanwhile beat egg white with remaining ¼ cup brown sugar until smooth. Stir in nuts and cinnamon. With small spatula spread on baked dough to cover completely. Bake on middle rack in oven 15 minutes longer or until top is firm to the touch. While still slightly warm, cut in 16 squares or 32 bars. Cool completely in pan on rack. Sprinkle with confectioners' sugar sifted through small strainer.

CINNAMON-NUT SQUARES

1 cup butter or
   margarine, softened
1 cup sugar
1 egg, separated
2 cups all-purpose
   flour, lightly
   spooned into cup

1 tablespoon
   cinnamon
¼ teaspoon salt
1 cup finely chopped
   pecans, filberts or
   unblanched
   almonds

Cream butter; gradually add sugar and continue creaming until light and fluffy. Add egg yolk, flour, cinnamon and salt and mix well. Spread in buttered 15 × 10 × 1-inch pan. Brush with lightly beaten egg white and sprinkle with nuts, then press nuts into surface. Bake in slow oven (300°F.) about 50 minutes. Cut in 48 squares while still hot. Store airtight in cool place. Good keepers and shippers.

BUTTER CHEWS

A double-decker delight.

¾ cup soft butter or
  margarine
3 tablespoons
  granulated sugar
1½ cups sifted flour
3 eggs, separated

2¼ cups light-brown
  sugar, packed
1 cup chopped nuts
¾ cup flaked coconut
Confectioners' sugar

Cream butter and granulated sugar. Blend in flour. Pat in bottom of 13 × 9 × 2-inch pan. Bake in moderate oven (350°F.) 15 minutes. Beat egg whites until stiff but not dry; set aside. Beat egg yolks until thick and lemon-colored. Beat in brown sugar. Stir in nuts and coconut. Fold in egg whites and spread over first mixture. Return to oven and bake 25 to 30 minutes longer. Cool and dust with confectioners' sugar. Cut in 20 bars about 4 × 2 inches.

OREGON FILBERT SQUARES

These crisp, buttery cookie squares laud the Oregon filbert. Easterners often call the same nuts hazelnuts. Washington and Oregon filbert growers, of course, say filberts used to be called hazelnuts and that filberts are an improvement on hazelnuts.

1 cup soft butter or
  margarine
1 cup sugar
1 egg, separated

2 cups all-purpose
  flour
¼ teaspoon ground
  cardamom
1 cup finely chopped
  filberts

Cream butter and sugar until light. Beat in egg yolk. Sift flour and cardamom; blend into creamed mixture. Spread dough evenly in 15 × 10 × 1-inch jelly roll pan. Press with palms to make a smooth surface. Beat egg white slightly; brush on dough. Sprinkle nuts evenly on surface, pressing into dough. Bake in very slow oven (275°F.) 1 hour. While hot, cut in 1½-inch squares. Cool. Makes about 70.

HUNGARIAN PECAN BARS

Like the Swedish Nut Bars, two layers are prepared separately and then baked together. Here the nuts are pecans.

1 cup flour	**2 egg yolks, divided**
⅛ teaspoon salt	**1½ teaspoons brandy**
¼ cup granulated	**Pecan Topping**
sugar	**Confectioners' sugar**
½ cup butter or	
margarine, softened	

Stir together flour, salt and granulated sugar. Cut in butter until mixture resembles coarse crumbs. Stir in 1 egg yolk and brandy; quickly mix with hands to form smooth dough. Press evenly into 9 × 9 × 2-inch baking pan, flouring fingers a little if necessary. Bake on bottom rack in preheated 350°F. oven 15 minutes or until firm *but not brown.* Brush with remaining egg yolk, slightly beaten, and spread with Pecan Topping. Bake on middle rack until light brown and firm, 15 to 20 minutes. Cool slightly on rack, then cut in bars. Sift with confectioners' sugar. Store airtight in cool, dry place. Makes 32.

PECAN TOPPING In heavy saucepan combine ¼ cup each packed brown sugar and granulated sugar, 2 egg whites and 1 teaspoon cinnamon. Stir over low heat until sugars dissolve, about 2 minutes. Remove from heat and stir in 2 cups finely chopped pecans until well blended.

DANISH MACAROON BARS
(Makronstaenger)

Ground almonds are the key ingredient.

1 cup sweet butter	**3 cups all-purpose**
¼ cup sugar	**flour (instant type**
2 to 3 tablespoons	**can be used)**
light cream	**⅔ cup confectioners'**
2 eggs, separated	**sugar**
	1 cup blanched
	almonds, ground

Cream butter and sugar until light. Add cream, beaten egg yolks and flour. Blend into a smooth dough. Roll out to a large oblong shape about ¼-inch thick. Beat 2 egg whites until stiff. Add ⅔ cup confectioners' sugar and 1 cup blanched and ground almonds. Spread on dough. Cut in bars about 2 inches × 1 inch. Put on greased cookie sheet. Bake in moderate oven (375°F.) 10 to 15 minutes. Makes about 5 dozen.

COFFEE-NUT BARS
(shown on plate 3)

An irresistible flavor combination.

1 cup flour
1 teaspoon baking
  powder
½ teaspoon cinnamon
¼ teaspoon salt
¼ cup butter or
  margarine, softened
⅔ cup packed brown
  sugar

1 egg
1 teaspoon vanilla
⅓ cup strong coffee
½ cup chopped nuts
Coffee Icing (recipe
  follows)

Mix well flour, baking powder, cinnamon and salt; set aside. In large bowl cream butter and sugar. Beat in egg and vanilla until fluffy. Alternately stir in flour mixture and coffee. Stir in nuts. Turn into greased 9 × 9 × 2-inch pan. Bake in preheated 350°F. oven 25 minutes or until pick inserted in center comes out clean. Cool in pan on rack. Spread with icing. Cut in 32 bars.

COFFEE ICING Stir until smooth 1 cup confectioners' sugar and 4 teaspoons strong coffee.

BLOND BROWNIES
(shown on plate 3)

Simple and delicious nut squares.

¾ cup flour
1 teaspoon baking
  powder
¼ teaspoon salt
¼ cup butter or
  margarine

1 cup packed light-
  brown sugar
1 egg
1 teaspoon vanilla
½ cup chopped nuts

Mix well flour, baking powder and salt; set aside. In saucepan melt butter; remove from heat. Stir in sugar until well mixed. Beat in egg and vanilla until blended. Stir in flour mixture, then nuts. Spread in greased 8 × 8 × 2-inch pan. Bake in preheated 350°F. oven 25 minutes or until pick inserted in center comes out clean. Cool in pan on rack. Cut in 32 squares.

DOUBLE-PEANUT BARS

(shown on plate 2)

Use unsalted peanuts if you prefer.

1 cup flour	¼ teaspoon salt
½ cup chopped salted peanuts	2 eggs
	⅔ cup sugar
1 teaspoon baking powder	½ cup peanut butter
	1 teaspoon vanilla

Mix well flour, peanuts, baking powder and salt; set aside. In bowl stir until well blended eggs, sugar, peanut butter and vanilla. Stir in flour mixture until well mixed. (Dough will be stiff.) Pat into greased 9 × 9 × 2-inch pan. Bake in preheated 350°F. oven 25 minutes or until pick inserted in center comes out clean. Cool in pan on rack. Cut in 24 bars.

PEANUT-BUTTER BROWNIES

Chewy and delicious. Chocolate bits add extra appeal but the flavor of peanuts prevails.

½ cup peanut butter (any style)	1 cup all-purpose flour
⅓ cup butter or margarine	1 teaspoon baking powder
1 cup sugar	¼ teaspoon salt
¼ cup packed brown sugar	1 package (6 ounces) semisweet chocolate pieces
2 eggs	½ teaspoon vanilla extract

Beat first 2 ingredients until blended. Gradually add sugars and beat until fluffy. Add eggs one at a time, beating well after each. Add dry ingredients and mix well. Stir in chocolate pieces and vanilla and spread in buttered 9-inch square pan. Bake in moderate oven (350°F.) 30 to 35 minutes. Cool in pan on cake rack. Then cut in 2¼-inch squares. Makes 16.

ORANGE PEANUT BARS

These moist, tender bars should be carefully removed from the pan.

2 cups flour
1 teaspoon baking
  soda
1 teaspoon baking
  powder
½ teaspoon salt
½ cup butter or
  margarine, softened
1 cup packed light-
  brown sugar
1 egg

2 teaspoons grated
  orange peel,
  divided
1 cup buttermilk
½ cup snipped pitted
  dates
½ cup coarsely
  chopped salted
  peanuts
⅓ cup orange juice
⅓ cup granulated
  sugar

Stir together flour, soda, baking powder and salt; set aside. In large bowl of mixer, cream butter, brown sugar, egg and 1 teaspoon grated orange peel until light and fluffy. Stir in flour mixture and buttermilk until well blended. Stir in dates and peanuts. Spread in greased 13 × 9 × 2-inch baking pan. Bake in preheated 375°F. oven 25 to 30 minutes, until golden brown. Cool in pan on rack. Reduce heat; simmer 5 minutes. Stir in remaining teaspoon orange peel. Spread evenly on top. Cool completely, then cut in 36 bars.

Oatmeal Bars

HONEY-GLOW BARS

This rich shortbread-type bar is an excellent take-along treat.

1½ cups flour
½ teaspoon salt
½ cup butter or
margarine, softened
½ cup plus 2
tablespoons
confectioners'
sugar, divided

1 teaspoon lemon
extract
2 tablespoons milk
1 cup uncooked oats
⅓ cup honey

Stir together flour and salt; set aside. In large bowl cream butter and ½ cup sugar until fluffy. Add lemon extract. Alternately add flour mixture with milk, beating well. Stir in oats until blended. (Dough will be quite stiff.) Press into greased 11 × 7 × 2-inch baking pan. Make wells in dough with back of spoon; drizzle evenly with honey. Bake in preheated 325°F. oven 25 to 30 minutes or until honey is absorbed. Cool in pan on rack. Cut in 24 bars. Sprinkle with remaining 2 tablespoons sugar.

NO-BAKE OATMEAL DANDIES
(shown on plate 6)

These make rich, tasty party bars for grown-ups, but kids love them too.

3 cups miniature
marshmallows
½ cup chunk-style
peanut butter
¼ cup honey

3 tablespoons butter
or margarine
1½ cups uncooked
oats
1 cup raisins

Line 9-inch square pan with foil; grease. In top of double boiler over hot (not boiling) water or in heavy saucepan over low heat cook marshmallows, peanut butter, honey and butter, stirring occasionally, until smooth. Remove from heat; stir in oats and raisins. Spread evenly in prepared pan; chill until firm. Remove from pan, then remove foil and cut in 36 squares.

OATMEAL-LEMONADE BARS
(shown on plate 7)

Prunes and lemon flavors blend together in a delicious filling.

FILLING:
1 package (12 ounces)
  pitted prunes,
  chopped
1 can (6 ounces)
  frozen lemonade
  concentrate,
  thawed, undiluted
1 lemonade-can water
¾ cup chopped
  walnuts or other
  nuts
⅓ cup sugar
¼ cup flour
½ teaspoon salt

CRUMB MIXTURE:
1¾ cups flour
1 teaspoon each
  baking soda and
  salt
¾ cup butter or
  margarine, softened
1 cup packed brown
  sugar
1¾ cups uncooked
  oats

FILLING In saucepan bring to boil prunes, lemonade concentrate and water. Reduce heat; cook 15 to 20 minutes or until consistency of purée. Stir in remaining ingredients.

CRUMB MIXTURE Stir together flour, soda and salt; set aside. In large bowl beat butter and sugar until creamy. Stir in flour mixture, then oats. Press half the crumb mixture into greased 13 × 9 × 2-inch baking pan; flatten. Evenly spread on filling. Sprinkle with remaining crumb mixture; pat lightly. Bake in preheated 400°F. oven 25 to 30 minutes or until lightly browned. Cool slightly in pan on rack. Cut in 36 bars and remove from pan to rack to cool completely.

OATMEAL-JELLY BARS
(shown on plate 3)

2 cups rolled oats
1 cup flour
¾ cup packed brown
  sugar

¼ teaspoon salt
¾ cup shortening
1 cup raspberry or
  preferred jelly

Mix well with fingertips oats, flour, sugar, salt and shortening. Pat half the mixture into bottom of greased 9 × 9 × 2-inch pan. Spread jelly evenly over dough. Sprinkle remaining dough over jelly. Lightly flatten with fingertips. Bake in preheated 350°F. oven 25 to 30 minutes or until golden. Cool in pan on rack. Cut in 24 bars.

OATMEAL SANDWICH

A light, moist cakelike cookie with a rich filling.

FILLING:
1 cup finely chopped
   dates
1 cup raisins
½ cup each dark corn
   syrup and boiling
   water
1 cup chopped
   walnuts

DOUGH:
2 cups flour
2 cups uncooked
   quick oats
1 teaspoon each
   baking powder and
   salt
½ teaspoon each
   cream of tartar and
   baking soda
1 cup butter or
   margarine, softened
1 cup packed brown
   sugar
2 eggs
½ cup sour cream

In small saucepan cook dates, raisins, corn syrup and water until mixture reaches consistency of jam. Remove from heat; stir in walnuts. Cool. Stir together flour, oats, baking powder, salt, cream of tartar and soda; set aside. In large bowl cream butter, sugar and eggs. Blend in sour cream. Stir in flour mixture until well blended. Spread half the dough in well-greased and floured 13 × 9 × 2-inch baking pan. Evenly spread on filling. Spread remaining dough evenly on top. Bake in preheated 350°F. oven 25 minutes or until well browned. Cool in pan on rack. Cut in 36 bars.

Spice Bars and Other Squares

JAN HAGEL

An exceptionally crisp Dutch cookie that is topped with sliced almonds.

1¼ cups flour
¾ cup sugar, divided
½ teaspoon cinnamon
½ cup cold sweet
    butter or margarine

1 egg, separated
½ cup sliced
    unblanched
    almonds

In large bowl combine flour, ½ cup sugar and the cinnamon. Cut in butter in small pieces. Work mixture with fingertips until small crumbs form. Add egg yolk and work in until well blended; shape dough in ball. Press evenly into well-greased 13 × 9 × 2-inch metal baking pan. Brush with slightly beaten egg white; sprinkle with remaining ¼ cup sugar and the almonds, pressing them into dough. Bake in preheated 350°F. oven 18 to 20 minutes or until lightly browned. Cool a few minutes, then cut in 2 × 1-inch bars. (A chef's knife or cleaver will cut neat slices; press blade down firmly through dough.) Finish cooling in pan on rack before removing cookies from pan. Makes 54.

PFEFFERNEUSSE SQUARES

An unusual bar version of a most popular holiday cookie.

1½ cups margarine
1½ cups sugar
½ cup molasses
¼ cup brandy or milk
8 drops anise oil
5½ cups sifted flour
1 teaspoon baking
    powder

½ teaspoon soda
2 teaspoons
    cinnamon
½ teaspoon each
    cloves and black
    pepper
1 teaspoon vanilla
Confectioners' sugar

Cream margarine; gradually beat in sugar. Add molasses, brandy and anise oil. Sift flour with baking powder, soda and spices; add to butter mixture with vanilla. Line a 13 × 9 × 2-inch pan with waxed paper; pound dough into pan. Refrigerate overnight. Invert pan on board and remove paper. Cut in 8 strips 1½ inches wide. Cut each strip in slices ¼ inch thick. Put on buttered cookie sheets. Bake in moderate oven (350°F.) about 10 minutes, or until done. Roll cookies in confectioners' sugar until well coated. Store in airtight container. Can be frozen. Makes about 168.

NUTMEG FLATS

During long, slow baking, the sugar and butter merge to rich brittleness.

1 cup butter or margarine, softened	2 cups flour
1 cup sugar	1½ teaspoons freshly grated or ground nutmeg
1 egg, separated	

In large bowl of mixer cream butter and sugar until fluffy. Add egg yolk and beat well. Stir in flour and nutmeg. Using small spatula or lightly floured fingertips, spread evenly in ungreased 15 × 10 × 1-inch jelly-roll pan. Beat egg white slightly and brush over top. Smooth surface with fingertips. Bake in preheated 275°F. oven until rich, golden brown, about 1 hour. While hot, cut in 2 × 3¾-inch bars; remove to racks to cool. Makes about 96.

SHORTBREAD FINGERS
(shown on plate 2)

1½ cups flour	margarine, softened
⅓ cup granulated sugar	½ teaspoon vanilla
½ cup butter or	Confectioners' sugar

Work flour, granulated sugar, butter and vanilla with fingers until blended. Press evenly into 8 × 8 × 2-inch pan. Prick well with fork. Bake in preheated 350°F. oven 25 minutes or until light golden. Cut in 32 bars, then sprinkle with confectioners' sugar. Cool completely in pan on rack.

GINGER SQUARES

An extra-spicy bar, with the special zest of ginger predominating.

½ cup butter or margarine	1½ teaspoons ginger, powdered or freshly grated	½ teaspoon cloves
½ cup sugar		1 teaspoon baking soda
2 eggs	1½ teaspoons cinnamon	½ teaspoon salt
1½ cups flour		½ cup molasses
		½ cup applesauce

In large bowl of mixer cream butter and sugar until fluffy. Beat in eggs. Stir in remaining ingredients until just blended. Bake in greased 8 × 8 × 2-inch pan in 350°F. oven 30 to 40 minutes or until pick inserted in center comes out clean. Serve warm or, if desired, cool in pan on rack, cut in 16 squares, wrap in foil, plastic wrap or sandwich bags and use for lunches. **NOTE:** Can be frozen up to 3 to 4 months.

IV
DROP COOKIES

Next to squares and bars, drop cookies are the easiest to make, and about the most versatile. Made from dough that is softer than that for rolled or molded cookies, drop cookies are placed individually in mounds or balls on a cookie sheet. Some of them hold their mound shape while baking; others spread out to become flat disks or crisp, lacy wafers.

While some dough can be neatly dropped onto a cookie sheet with one spoon, it is generally wiser to use two spoons to make drop cookies—one to pick up dough, the other to transfer it onto the sheet. That way, the cookies will be uniform in shape and cook evenly in the oven.

Certain drop cookie recipes specify another method of forming: measuring the dough out by the teaspoonful and rolling it into little balls by hand before placing it on sheets.

Still others are placed onto sheets with spoons and then flattened with a fork, spoon or bottom of a drinking glass.

Unless the recipe gives other instructions for spacing, be sure to leave at least two inches between each teaspoon mound of cookie dough. The cookies with proportionately more butter and sugar than flour will always spread.

The assembly-line method of baking (see page 12) is ideal for cooking quantities of drop cookies.

Oatmeal Cookies

ALMOND OATMEAL COOKIES

A fresh and different taste combination.

¾ cup margarine,
  softened
1 cup packed brown
  sugar
1 teaspoon almond
  extract
1 cup all-purpose
  flour
½ teaspoon each
  baking soda and
  salt
2 cups quick-cooking
  rolled oats (not
  instant)
½ cup finely chopped
  blanched almonds

Beat first 3 ingredients and 3 tablespoons water together until smooth. Mix flour, soda and salt and stir into mixture. Add oats and nuts and mix well with spoon or hands. Drop by teaspoonfuls onto greased cookie sheets and press down slightly. Bake in preheated 350°F. oven 12 to 14 minutes. Makes about 5 dozen.

PINEAPPLE-OATMEAL COOKIES

½ cup soft butter or
  margarine
½ cup granulated
  sugar
½ cup brown sugar,
  packed
1 egg
1 can (about 9
  ounces) crushed
  pineapple (see note)
1½ cups rolled oats
1 cup sifted flour
½ teaspoon baking
  soda
½ teaspoon salt
½ teaspoon cinnamon
Dash nutmeg
½ cup chopped
  walnuts

Cream butter; add sugars and beat until light. Add egg and beat well. Add pineapple, oats, sifted dry ingredients and nuts; mix well. Drop by teaspoonfuls onto ungreased cookie sheets. Bake in moderate oven (375°F.) about 15 minutes. Makes about 4 dozen. **NOTE:** You can use fresh pineapple, finely chopped, and increase granulated sugar to ¾ cup.

ALL-AMERICAN OATMEAL CRISPS
(shown on plate 7)

Leave plenty of room on baking sheets for these to spread.

1¼ cups flour	½ cup granulated
1 teaspoon baking	sugar
powder	2 eggs
½ teaspoon each	¼ cup milk
baking soda and	1 teaspoon vanilla
salt	3 cups uncooked oats
1 cup butter or	1 cup semisweet
margarine, softened	chocolate pieces
1 cup packed brown	
sugar	

Stir together flour, baking powder, soda and salt; set aside. In large bowl beat butter and sugars until creamy. Beat in eggs, milk and vanilla until well blended. Stir in flour mixture, then oats and chocolate. Drop by rounded teaspoonfuls 1½ to 2 inches apart on greased baking sheets. Bake in preheated 350°F. oven 12 to 15 minutes or until lightly browned. Remove to rack to cool. Makes 84.

OATMEAL-PECAN CRISPS Prepare batter as above but substitute ¾ cup chopped pecans for chocolate pieces.

OATMEAL-COCONUT CRISPS Prepare batter as above but substitute ¾ cup flaked or shredded coconut for chocolate pieces.

OATMEAL LACE COOKIES

Delicate and rich. Served with vanilla ice cream, the ideal dessert for a special dinner.

2¼ cups quick-	1 cup butter melted
cooking rolled oats	1 egg, slightly beaten
2¼ cups packed light-	1 teaspoon vanilla or
brown sugar	almond extract
3 tablespoons flour	
1 teaspoon salt	

Mix all ingredients. Drop by level measuring-teaspoonfuls onto well-buttered cookie sheets. Bake in moderate oven (375°F.) about 5 minutes, watching closely. Let cool a moment before removing from cookie sheet. Makes about 120.

COCONUT CRISPS
(shown on plate 7)

Like all crisp oatmeal cookies these spread, so leave plenty of room on baking sheets.

1 cup flour	1⅔ cups sugar
1 teaspoon each baking powder and salt	2 eggs
	1½ teaspoons vanilla
½ teaspoon baking soda	2½ cups uncooked quick oats
¾ cup butter or margarine, softened	1 cup flaked coconut

Stir together flour, baking powder, salt and soda; set aside. In large bowl cream butter and sugar until light. Beat in eggs one at a time. Stir in flour mixture, vanilla and oats, then coconut. Drop by teaspoonfuls 3 inches apart on ungreased baking sheets. Bake in preheated 375°F. oven 10 to 15 minutes or until lightly browned. Cool on rack. Makes 60.

SWEDISH COCONUT OATMEAL COOKIES
(Kokos-Havrekakor)

Nuts give a special texture and flavor to these popular cookies. Use walnuts, pecans or almonds—whichever your fancy.

1 cup shredded coconut	1 egg, beaten
½ cup butter or margarine	1 teaspoon vanilla
	1 cup quick-cooking rolled oats
1 cup packed brown sugar	½ cup chopped nuts

Put coconut in a shallow pan and toast in a slow oven (325°F.) until delicately browned. Stir occasionally. Cool and crush with rolling pin. Cream butter. Add sugar and cream together thoroughly. Add egg and vanilla and beat until light and fluffy. Add oats, nuts and coconut. Drop by teaspoonfuls onto greased cookie sheet. Flatten each cookie with the bottom of a small glass dipped in flour. Bake in moderate oven (375°F.) 6 to 8 minutes. Makes about 4 dozen.

GRANDMA'S FAVORITE OATMEAL COOKIES

(shown on plates 6 and 7)

A fresh apple slice in the cookie jar keeps these family pleasers soft.

1¾ cups flour	2 eggs
1 teaspoon each baking soda, salt and cinnamon	2 cups uncooked quick oats
½ cup shortening	1 cup raisins
1¼ cups sugar	½ cup chopped walnuts or other
⅓ cup light molasses	nuts

Stir together flour, baking soda, salt and cinnamon; set aside. In large bowl cream shortening, sugar, molasses and eggs until fluffy. Stir in flour mixture, then oats, raisins and walnuts. Drop by rounded teaspoonfuls 1½ to 2 inches apart on greased baking sheets. Bake in preheated 400°F. oven 10 to 12 minutes or until lightly browned. Remove to rack to cool. Makes 60.

OATMEAL COOKIES

Dough can be prepared a day ahead and refrigerated. Recipe can also be halved.

2 cups shortening (butter, margarine or vegetable shortening or half each of any two)	4 eggs	1 to 2 cups chopped nuts, semisweet chocolate pieces, raisins or coconut
	2 teaspoons vanilla	
	3¼ cups flour stirred with 1½ teaspoons salt and 1 teaspoon each baking powder and baking soda	
2 cups packed brown sugar		(or any 2 of these; if using coconut, use almond extract instead of vanilla)
1½ cups granulated sugar	6½ cups rolled oats	

In large bowl of mixer beat shortening and sugars until creamy; add eggs and vanilla and beat until thoroughly mixed. At low speed beat in flour mixture. (If necessary, transfer mixture to 4-quart Dutch oven or bowl.) With wooden spoon stir in oats and nuts. (If preferred, cover and refrigerate dough overnight.) Drop by teaspoonfuls on lightly greased cookie sheets about 1 inch apart. Bake on top rack in preheated 300°F. oven 20 to 25 minutes or until lightly browned around edges (centers will be soft). Cool on cookie sheets 10 minutes; remove to rack. Makes 20 dozen.

CRUNCHY OAT COOKIES

With bran, wheat germ, oats, walnuts and an extra helping of protein from the nonfat dry milk, these cookies are as wholesome as they are tasty. Kids love them—great in lunch boxes and for after-school snacks. They can even provide quick breakfast nourishment for late risers.

1 cup whole-wheat flour
⅓ cup nonfat dry milk
¼ cup toasted wheat germ
¼ cup unprocessed bran
1 teaspoon baking soda
1 teaspoon baking powder
½ teaspoon salt
1 teaspoon cinnamon
¼ teaspoon nutmeg
⅛ teaspoon ground cloves
1 cup butter or margarine, softened
1 cup packed brown sugar
2 eggs
2 cups rolled oats
½ cup chopped walnuts
½ cup raisins or currants

Stir together flour, dry milk, wheat germ, bran, soda, baking powder, salt and spices; set aside. In large bowl of mixer cream butter and sugar. Add eggs; beat until fluffy. Gradually stir in flour mixture just to blend. Stir in oats, walnuts and raisins until well blended. Drop by rounded teaspoonfuls about 2 inches apart on greased cookie sheets. Bake in preheated 350°F. oven 9 to 10 minutes or until light brown. Remove to racks to cool. Makes about 84.

ORANGE GRANOLA COOKIES

Better double this batch—these cookies go fast.

2 cups flour
2½ teaspoons baking powder
1½ teaspoons cinnamon
½ teaspoon each baking soda and salt
¼ teaspoon ground cloves
½ cup butter or margarine, softened
½ cup sugar
1 egg
⅓ cup frozen orange-juice concentrate, thawed, undiluted
½ cup honey
1 cup raisins
1 cup uncooked oats
½ cup sunflower seeds

Stir together flour, baking powder, cinnamon, soda, salt and cloves; set aside. In large bowl cream butter and sugar until light and fluffy. Beat in egg. Alternately stir in flour mixture, orange concentrate and honey until blended. Stir in raisins, oats and sunflower seeds. Drop by tablespoonfuls 2 inches apart on greased baking sheets. Bake in preheated 350°F. oven 15 to 20 minutes or until lightly browned. Cool on rack. Makes 48.

TRAILSIDE OATMEAL TREATS
(shown on plates 6 and 7)

There's a pleasant surprise for peanut-butter lovers in these chunky cookies.

1¾ cups flour
1 teaspoon baking
   soda
½ teaspoon salt
½ cup butter or
   margarine, softened
½ cup chunk-style
   peanut butter
1 cup granulated
   sugar

1 cup packed brown
   sugar
2 eggs
¼ cup milk
1 teaspoon vanilla
2½ cups uncooked
   oats
½ cup each
   semisweet
   chocolate pieces
   and raisins

Stir together flour, soda and salt; set aside. In large bowl beat butter, peanut butter and sugars until creamy. Beat in eggs, milk and vanilla. Stir in flour mixture, then oats, chocolate pieces and raisins. Drop by rounded tablespoonfuls 3 inches apart on ungreased baking sheets. Bake in preheated 350°F. oven about 15 minutes or until lightly browned. Remove to rack to cool. Makes 42.

DOUBLE-TREAT WALNUT COOKIES
(shown on plate 6)

These nutritious cookies are marvelous for after-school snacks with milk.

1 cup whole-wheat
   flour
¼ cup each nonfat
   dry milk and wheat
   germ
1 teaspoon each salt
   and baking powder
¼ teaspoon cinnamon

¾ cup shortening (see
   Note)
1¼ cups packed
   brown sugar
1 egg
¼ cup frozen orange-
   juice concentrate,
   thawed, undiluted

1½ cups uncooked
   quick oats
1 cup chopped
   walnuts
½ cup chopped
   raisins
2 tablespoons
   granulated sugar

Stir together flour, milk, wheat germ, salt, baking powder and cinnamon; set aside. In large bowl cream shortening, brown sugar and egg until fluffy; add orange concentrate. Stir in flour mixture, then oats, walnuts and raisins. Drop by heaping tablespoonfuls 4 inches apart on lightly greased baking sheets. Press with bottom of glass dipped in sugar to 3¼-inch diameter. Bake in preheated 350°F. oven about 15 minutes or until cookie springs back when pressed lightly. Let stand 2 to 3 minutes. Remove to rack and cool completely. Makes 22.
NOTE: For richer flavor substitute butter for half the shortening.

Chocolate and Combination Chocolate Cookies

GIANT CHOCOLATE CRACKLES

Extrachocolaty and extra delicious.

2 cups flour
2 teaspoons baking
  powder
½ teaspoon salt
½ cup butter or
  margarine, softened
2 cups sugar

4 squares (4 ounces)
  unsweetened
  chocolate, melted
  and cooled
4 eggs
2 teaspoons vanilla

Mix well flour, baking powder and salt; set aside. In large bowl of mixer cream butter and sugar until light. Beat in chocolate until blended. Add eggs and vanilla; beat until light and fluffy. Gradually stir in flour mixture until well blended. Chill dough well. Using heaping tablespoonfuls of dough, shape in balls. Place 3 inches apart on greased cookie sheets. Bake in preheated 350°F. oven 25 minutes or until top of cookie springs back when lightly pressed with finger. Remove to racks to cool. Makes about 24 large cookies.

RICH CHOCOLATE DROPS

Extra rich, easy to make.

½ cup butter, melted
½ teaspoon salt
1 teaspoon vanilla
1 cup sugar
2 eggs, beaten

3 squares (3 ounces)
  unsweetened
  chocolate, melted
  and cooled
¾ cup all-purpose
  flour
½ teaspoon soda

Mix all ingredients together. Drop by teaspoonfuls onto cookie sheets. Bake in moderate oven (375°F.) 8 to 10 minutes. Makes about 4 dozen.

CHOCOLATE-OATMEAL COOKIES

Cocoa gives a special flavor and texture to these hearty and delicious cookies.

¾ cup flour
1 teaspoon baking
  soda
⅓ cup chopped
  almonds or nuts
½ cup butter or
  margarine, softened
1 cup packed brown
  sugar

1 egg
¼ cup unsweetened
  cocoa
1 teaspoon vanilla
1½ cups quick-
  cooking oatmeal
Blanched whole
  almonds (optional)

Stir together flour, soda and chopped almonds; set aside. With mixer cream butter and sugar until fluffy. Add egg, cocoa and vanilla and beat until well blended. Add oatmeal and flour mixture and mix until well blended. Drop by heaping teaspoonfuls about 2 inches apart on greased cookie sheets. Press whole almond onto each cookie. Bake in preheated 350°F. oven 15 minutes or until crisp and light-brown on bottoms. Remove to rack to cool. Makes about 36.

SWEDISH CHOCOLATE OATMEAL DROPS
(Chokladhavrekakor)

Richer, and crisper, than most drop cookies.

1 cup shortening
¾ cup sugar
1 egg, beaten
3 tablespoons cocoa

½ cup all-purpose
  flour
2½ cups quick-
  cooking rolled oats

Melt shortening and cool. Add sugar and beat until light. Add egg, cocoa, flour and oats. Drop by teaspoonfuls onto greased cookie sheet. Bake in moderate oven (350°F.) about 12 minutes. Makes about 5 dozen.

MOCHA CHIP COOKIES

½ cup butter,
  softened
½ cup packed light-
  brown sugar
1 egg, beaten
½ teaspoon baking
  soda
2 teaspoons very
  strong coffee

1 cup all-purpose
  flour
1 package (6 ounces)
  semisweet
  chocolate pieces
½ cup chopped
  almonds

Cream butter and sugar until well blended. Add remaining ingredients and mix well. Preheat oven to 350°F. Drop dough, one tablespoon at a time, onto lightly greased cookie sheet, leaving plenty of room between cookies (drop first cookie to see how far it spreads before doing next one). Bake cookies 9 to 10 minutes, then remove from oven and slip onto cake rack to cool. Pack finished cookies in tin box for transfer to picnic basket. Makes about 2 dozen.

DANISH CHOCOLATE COOKIES
(Chokoladekager)

2 squares (2 ounces)
  unsweetened
  chocolate
½ cup butter or
  margarine
1 cup packed light-
  brown sugar
1 egg, beaten

3 cups all-purpose
  flour (instant type
  can be used)
½ teaspoon salt
½ teaspoon soda
¾ cup sweet milk or
  buttermilk
Vanilla Frosting

Melt chocolate with butter. Add brown sugar and beaten egg. Sift flour, salt and soda together and add alternately with milk to first mixture. Drop by teaspoonfuls onto greased cookie sheet. Bake in moderate oven (375°F.) about 12 minutes. When cool, spread with **Vanilla Frosting.** To make, mix confectioners' sugar and enough cream to make of spreading consistency. Flavor with vanilla. Chocolate shot can be sprinkled on top. Makes about 50.

CHOCOLATE WALNUT DROP COOKIES

Delicious as is or make sandwich cookies (see Note).

½ cup butter or margarine, softened	2 squares (2 ounces) unsweetened chocolate, melted and cooled
1 cup sugar	1 cup flour
2 eggs	½ cup chopped walnuts
1 teaspoon vanilla	Confectioners' sugar
⅛ teaspoon salt	

In large bowl of mixer cream butter, sugar, eggs, vanilla and salt until fluffy. Beat in chocolate until well blended. Stir in flour and nuts. Drop by heaping teaspoonfuls 2 inches apart on well-greased cookie sheet. Bake in preheated 350°F. oven 10 minutes or until edges are crisp. Cool 1 minute before removing to rack to cool. Sift confectioners' sugar over tops. Makes about 4 dozen. **NOTE:** To make sandwich cookies fill 2 cookies with 1 to 2 teaspoons Creamy Chocolate Frosting.

Creamy Chocolate Frosting

Can be prepared ahead and refrigerated up to 1 week.

2 teaspoons cornstarch	⅛ teaspoon salt
½ cup water	1 package (6 ounces) semisweet chocolate pieces
1 can (5⅓ ounces) evaporated milk (⅔ cup)	1 teaspoon vanilla or rum extract
2 tablespoons butter or margarine	

In small heavy saucepan cook and stir cornstarch, water, milk, butter and salt over low heat until thickened and smooth; remove from heat. Stir in chocolate until melted, returning to low heat if necessary. Stir in vanilla. Chill until thickened and of spreading consistency. Store covered in refrigerator. Stir before using. Good on cupcakes, as filling for layer cake or jelly roll or to sandwich crisp cookies. Keeps about 1 week. Makes 1½ cups.

COCONUT-BROWNIE DROPS

½ cup butter or
   margarine
3 squares (3 ounces)
   unsweetened
   chocolate

1½ cups sugar
5 eggs
1½ cups flour
1 cup shredded
   coconut

In medium saucepan melt butter and chocolate over low heat, stirring constantly. Remove from heat. Stir in sugar. Beat in eggs one at a time until well blended. Stir in flour and coconut. Chill dough at least 2 hours. Drop by heaping teaspoonfuls 2 inches apart on greased cookie sheets. Flatten slightly with back of spoon. Bake in preheated 350°F. oven 10 to 12 minutes or until cookie springs back when pressed lightly with finger. Remove to rack to cool. Makes about 6 dozen cookies.

CHOCOLATE PEANUT MACAROONS

*The crusty outside and slightly moist and hollow inside
make these a real treat.*

2 egg whites, at room
   temperature
⅛ teaspoon cream of
   tartar
½ cup sugar

½ teaspoon vanilla
1 package (6 ounces)
   semisweet
   chocolate pieces,
   melted and cooled
½ cup chopped salted
   peanuts

In small bowl of mixer beat egg whites and cream of tartar until almost stiff. Gradually beat in sugar until very stiff. Add vanilla. Gently fold in chocolate, leaving a marbled effect, then peanuts. Drop by teaspoonfuls onto greased cookie sheets. Bake in preheated 350°F. oven about 10 minutes. Remove carefully to racks to cool. Makes about 30.

CHOCOLATE PEANUT-BUTTER DROPS

They contain spices and oatmeal, too.

¼ cup each soft
   shortening and
   peanut butter
½ cup sugar
1 egg
¾ cup sifted flour
¼ teaspoon soda
½ teaspoon salt

⅛ teaspoon nutmeg
¼ teaspoon cinnamon
¼ cup water
½ cup rolled oats
1 package (6 ounces)
   semisweet
   chocolate pieces

Cream shortening, peanut butter and sugar until light. Beat in egg. Add sifted dry ingredients and water; mix well. Fold in oats and chocolate. Drop from teaspoon on sheet. Bake in moderate oven (375°F.) about 12 minutes. While still warm, roll in sugar. Makes about 4 dozen. (Good keepers and shippers.)

CHOCOLATE PECAN CRINKLES

These make fine gifts and can be shipped. They'll keep fresh a week or two. Cookies contain no flour.

¼ cup butter (not
   whipped)
¾ cup packed light-
   brown sugar
½ cup semisweet
   chocolate pieces or
   3 squares (3 ounces)

semisweet chocolate
1 cup pecans, grated,
   finely ground or
   whirled in blender
1 egg
1 teaspoon vanilla

In a heavy saucepan, melt butter and sugar and stir until sugar dissolves and mixture begins to boil around the edges. Add the chocolate and heat gently until chocolate is melted and blended, stirring constantly. Remove from heat and stir in pecans. Add egg and vanilla and beat to form a thick paste. You can whip the whole batter in a blender until thoroughly smooth or use the batter as is. Lightly butter a sheet of foil fitted over a cookie sheet. Drop the batter by rounded teaspoonfuls onto the foil, leaving 2 inches between cookies because they spread when baking. Bake in moderate oven (350°F.) 10 to 12 minutes. Chill as soon as removed from oven. When cold, remove at once from foil and store airtight. Makes about 3 dozen.

WASPS' NESTS

Wonderfully light, meringue-type cookies.

1 cup granulated
  sugar
½ cup water
1 pound unblanched
  almonds, slivered
5 egg whites
⅛ teaspoon salt

1 teaspoon vanilla
1 pound
  confectioners'
  sugar
4 squares (4 ounces)
  unsweetened
  chocolate, melted

Cook granulated sugar and water until syrup spins a thread (234°F. on a candy thermometer). Add nuts slowly and continue stirring until all syrup is absorbed. Beat egg whites until frothy; add salt and vanilla; continue beating until whites are very stiff; gradually beat in confectioners' sugar. Fold in nuts and chocolate. Drop from teaspoon on well-buttered cookie sheets. Bake in moderate oven (300°F.) 20 to 25 minutes. Can be frozen. Makes 120.

BRANDY SAND TARTS

Simple, but delicious.

1 cup soft butter or
  margarine
1 cup sugar
2 tablespoons brandy
1 egg

1 package (6 ounces)
  semisweet
  chocolate pieces,
  ground
2 cups sifted flour
⅛ teaspoon salt

Cream butter and sugar with brandy until light. Beat in egg. Add remaining ingredients and mix well. Drop by teaspoonfuls on ungreased cookie sheets and bake in moderate oven (350°F.) about 15 minutes. Makes about 7 dozen.

Fruit Cookies

A bountiful harvest—and from the vegetable garden, carrots and zucchini in two marvelous recipes.

OLD-FASHIONED APPLE COOKIES

½ cup butter,
  softened
1⅓ cups packed
  brown sugar
1 egg
¼ cup apple juice
1 cup finely chopped
  peeled cored apples
2 cups whole-wheat
  pastry flour
½ teaspoon salt

1 teaspoon baking
  soda
½ teaspoon ground
  cloves
1 teaspoon cinnamon
1 cup unsulfured
  raisins
1 cup chopped
  walnuts or other
  nuts
Glaze (optional)

Cream butter and sugar until blended. Add egg and beat well. Beat in juice. Add next 5 ingredients and mix well. Then fold in remaining ingredients, except glaze. Drop by rounded teaspoonfuls about 2 inches apart on greased baking sheets. Bake in preheated 375°F. oven about 13 minutes. Remove to racks and, if desired, brush with glaze while still warm. Makes 48.

Glaze Mix well ½ cup confectioners' sugar, 1 tablespoon softened butter and 2 tablespoons apple juice (or enough to make a thin glaze).

CURRANT DROPS

1 cup butter or
  margarine, softened
1 cup sugar
1 egg, slightly beaten
1 teaspoon vanilla

1 teaspoon grated
  lemon rind
1 cup currants,
  scalded and well
  drained
2⅓ cups sifted cake
  flour

Cream butter. Gradually add sugar and beat until fluffy. Add remaining ingredients and mix well. Drop by level measuring-teaspoonfuls 2 inches apart on well-greased cookie sheet. Bake in moderate oven (375°F.) 10 minutes, or until golden and lightly browned around the edges. Remove at once to rack. Cool and store airtight. Makes about 7 dozen.

RAISIN-CARROT COOKIES

Inexpensive and available year round, carrots are naturally sweet and nutritious. These soft, cakelike cookies provide all the daily requirements of Vitamin A for children and adults.

½ cup shortening
1 cup packed brown sugar
3 eggs
1 cup grated carrot
2 cups flour
1 teaspoon baking powder
½ teaspoon each baking soda and
cinnamon
1½ cups raisins
½ cup coarsely chopped nuts
⅓ cup milk
⅓ cup undiluted orange juice concentrate
1 teaspoon vanilla

In large bowl of mixer beat shortening, sugar and eggs. Stir in carrot; set aside. Mix flour, baking powder, soda and cinnamon; stir in raisins and nuts. Add with milk to carrot mixture. Stir in orange concentrate and vanilla. Drop by teaspoonfuls 2 inches apart on greased cookie sheet. Bake in preheated 350°F. oven 10 to 12 minutes or until lightly browned around edges. Remove to rack; cool. Makes about 96.

CRANBERRY DROP COOKIES

Tart and delicious.

½ cup butter or margarine
1 cup granulated sugar
¾ cup packed brown sugar
¼ cup milk
2 tablespoons orange juice
1 egg
2⅓ cups all-purpose flour
1 teaspoon baking powder
¼ teaspoon baking soda
½ teaspoon salt
1 cup chopped nuts
2½ cups coarsely chopped cranberries

Cream butter and sugars together. Beat in the milk, orange juice and egg. Mix together next 4 ingredients. Add to creamed mixture and mix well. Stir in nuts and cranberries. Drop by teaspoonfuls onto greased baking sheet. Bake in moderate oven (375°F.) about 12 minutes. Makes about 6½ dozen.

RAW-APPLE COOKIES
(shown on plate 7)

A great soft cookie that keeps well. The red apple peel is an attractive addition, while the sunflower nuts add crunch.

1½ cups flour
½ teaspoon each salt,
  baking powder,
  baking soda,
  cinnamon and
  ground cloves
½ cup dry-roasted
  sunflower nuts
  (see Note)
½ cup shortening

1 cup packed brown
  sugar
2 eggs
1 cup uncooked
  quick oats
1¾ cups chopped tart
  red cooking apples
  (2 large)
½ cup each plumped
  raisins and chopped
  pitted dates

Stir together flour, salt, baking powder, soda, cinnamon, cloves and sunflower nuts; set aside. In large bowl beat shortening and sugar until creamy. Beat in eggs until well blended. Stir in flour mixture, then oats, apples, raisins and dates. Drop by well-rounded teaspoonfuls 1½ to 2 inches apart on greased baking sheets. Bake in preheated 350°F. oven 12 to 15 minutes or until lightly browned. Remove to rack to cool. **NOTE:** Substitute ½ cup chopped walnuts if desired.

COCONUT COOKIES

Great for gift-giving.

1 cup granulated
  sugar
½ cup packed brown
  sugar
½ cup shortening
2 eggs
1 teaspoon salt

1 teaspoon baking
  soda
1 teaspoon vanilla
2 cups flour
1 cup shredded
  coconut
1 tablespoon water

With spoon stir sugars, shortening, eggs, salt, soda and vanilla until smooth; add remaining ingredients and mix well. Drop by rounded ½ teaspoonfuls about 1 inch apart on lightly greased cookie sheets. Bake in preheated 375°F. oven 7 to 8 minutes or until tops are firm and cookies are golden brown. Cool on racks. Cookies are crisp. Store in airtight container up to 3 weeks. Makes 10 to 11 dozen.

LEMON-COCONUT CRISPS

½ cup butter or
  margarine, softened
½ cup sugar
1 egg, separated
Juice and grated rind
  of 1 lemon
⅓ cup flaked coconut

1 cup all-purpose
  flour
½ teaspoon baking
  soda
1 teaspoon cream of
  tartar
Candied fruit, nut
  halves

Cream butter and sugar. Beat in egg yolk and lemon juice and rind. Add coconut. Sift dry ingredients and add to creamed mixture. Using measuring-teaspoonful of batter, drop small balls onto greased cookie sheet. Brush lightly with unbeaten egg white and sprinkle with small amount of sugar. Decorate tops with small piece of candied fruit or nut half and bake in moderate oven (350°F.) 12 to 15 minutes. Makes 7 dozen.

LEMON-NUT CRISPS

½ cup butter or
  margarine
1 cup sugar
1 egg
2 tablespoons water
1½ teaspoons grated
  lemon peel
1 tablespoon lemon
  juice

1¾ cups flour
1 teaspoon baking
  powder
½ teaspoon baking
  soda
½ teaspoon salt
¾ cup chopped nuts

In large bowl of mixer cream butter and sugar until fluffy. Beat in egg, water, lemon peel and juice. Gradually beat in flour, baking powder, baking soda and salt. Stir in nuts. Drop by heaping teaspoonfuls 2 inches apart on greased cookie sheets. Bake in preheated 375°F. oven 10 to 12 minutes or until golden around edges. Remove to racks to cool. Makes about 5 dozen.

SHERRY CHRISTMAS TREES

Spanish cookies with a delightful lemon and wine flavor.

1½ cups unsifted flour	1 egg, beaten
½ cup white sugar	2 tablespoons sherry
½ teaspoon salt	1 egg white, slightly beaten
Grated rind 1 lemon	Green sugar
¼ cup olive oil	

Mix all ingredients, except egg white and green sugar, together thoroughly. Roll ⅛-inch thick and cut with small Christmas-tree cutter. Put on sheet and brush with egg white; sprinkle with green sugar. Bake in hot oven (400°F.) about 10 minutes. Makes 48. (Good keepers and shippers.)

ORANGE LACE COOKIES

1 cup soft butter	½ teaspoon vanilla
⅔ cup sugar	½ cup sifted flour
2 eggs	½ teaspoon salt
1 teaspoon grated orange rind	1 cup rolled oats
	½ cup flaked coconut

Cream butter; gradually beat in sugar. Add eggs, one at a time, beating well after each addition. Add orange rind and vanilla. Sift flour with salt; add to butter mixture. Stir in oats and coconut. Drop by half teaspoonfuls on buttered cookie sheets; flatten with a silver or stainless-steel knife dipped in cold water, or press with bottom of glass dipped in flour. Bake in moderate oven (350°F.) 10 to 12 minutes, or until edges are lightly browned. Store in airtight container. Can be frozen. Makes 96.

PINEAPPLE DROP COOKIES

½ cup butter or margarine	¾ cup undrained crushed pineapple	½ teaspoon soda
1 cup light-brown sugar, packed	2 cups sifted flour	½ teaspoon salt
1 egg	1 teaspoon baking powder	½ cup each seedless raisins and chopped nuts
1 teaspoon vanilla		

Cream butter until light and fluffy. Gradually add sugar and beat well. Beat in egg and vanilla. Stir in pineapple, sifted dry ingredients, raisins and nuts. Drop by teaspoonfuls onto greased cookie sheets and bake in moderate oven (375°F.) 12 minutes, or until lightly browned. Makes 54.

LEMON-ZUCCHINI COOKIES

Delicate, soft cookies.

2 cups flour
1 teaspoon baking
  powder
½ teaspoon salt
¾ cup butter or
  margarine
¾ cup sugar

1 egg, beaten
1 teaspoon (or more)
  grated lemon peel
1 cup shredded
  unpeeled zucchini
1 cup chopped
  walnuts
Lemon Frost (recipe
  follows; optional)

Stir together flour, baking powder and salt; set aside. In large bowl of mixer cream butter and sugar until light. Beat in egg and peel until fluffy. At low speed or with rubber scraper stir in flour mixture until dough is smooth. Stir in zucchini and walnuts. Drop by rounded teaspoonfuls on greased cookie sheets. Bake in preheated 375°F. oven 15 to 20 minutes or until very lightly browned. While warm, drizzle lightly with Lemon Frost. Cool on racks. Makes 72 to 84.

LEMON FROST Mix well 1 cup confectioners' sugar and 1½ tablespoons lemon juice.

Nut Cookies

ALMOND-LACE COOKIES

Crisp and very tender.

1 cup finely chopped blanched almonds	½ cup sugar
½ cup butter or margarine, softened	2 tablespoons flour
	2 tablespoons milk

Cook and stir all ingredients in 2-quart saucepan over medium heat just until butter melts and all ingredients are well blended. Drop by level measuring-teaspoons onto well-greased floured cookie sheets, leaving 3-inch space between cookies. Bake in preheated 350°F. oven 5 to 6 minutes, or until lightly browned and glossy. Cool on sheets a few minutes until firm enough to remove to rack. Store airtight in cool place with plastic between layers. Makes about 4 dozen.

ALMOND MACAROONS

Italy's most popular cookie.

Combine 2 cups blanched almonds, ground fine and very dry, 1 cup sifted granulated sugar, 2 egg whites, beaten stiff, and 1 teaspoon almond extract. Blend together gently but thoroughly, and drop batter by teaspoonfuls on well-greased and floured cookie sheets leaving 2 inches' space between each. Sprinkle with confectioners' sugar. Let stand at room temperature 2 hours to dry. Bake in slow oven (300°F.) 15 to 20 minutes, or until golden. Cool on cookie sheet 1 or 2 minutes before removing. To decorate for Christmas, press half a red or green candied cherry or a cinnamon candy into each macaroon while still hot. Makes 20 to 30, depending on size.

Jam-Filled Macaroons: Mix batter as in above recipe. Drop ½ teaspoon on cookie sheet. Make small indenture in middle and fill with ¼ teaspoon raspberry jam. Cover with remaining half teaspoon batter and flatten out with fork. Sprinkle with sugar and proceed as above.

FLORENTINES

A delicate, elegant cookie, also from Italy.

Combine ½ cup heavy cream, 3 tablespoons butter and ½ cup sugar in saucepan and bring to boil. Remove from heat and stir in 1¼ cups finely chopped almonds, ⅓ cup sifted flour and ¾ cup finely chopped candied orange peel. Drop by tablespoonfuls on greased and floured cookie sheet, keeping cookies 3 inches apart. Bake in moderate oven (350°F.) about 10 minutes. Cool 5 minutes. Remove carefully with spatula to cake rack. Cool. Spiral melted chocolate over cookie tops and decorate with tiny colored candies. Makes about 2 dozen 3-inch cookies.

ITALIAN CENCI

La Befana, the Italian Santa Claus, brings these almond-flavored cookies to good children.

3 eggs	1½ teaspoons baking
2 tablespoons	powder
granulated sugar	1½ teaspoons
½ teaspoon salt	softened butter
½ teaspoon vanilla	Fat for frying
½ teaspoon almond	2 tablespoons
extract	confectioners'
2 cups sifted flour	sugar
	⅛ teaspoon cinnamon

Beat eggs, granulated sugar and salt until frothy. Add vanilla and almond extracts. Sift flour with baking powder. Add gradually to egg mixture. Add butter. Mix well. Turn out on lightly floured board and knead about 10 minutes. Divide dough in half. Roll to noodle thinness. Cut in ¾-inch strips with a fluted pastry wheel. Fry in hot, deep fat (370°F. on frying thermometer) about 1 minute. Drain; sprinkle with mixed confectioners' sugar and cinnamon. Makes 4 dozen.

PEANUT BUTTEROONS

They're just peanut butter, sugar and egg whites.

Gradually beat ⅔ cup confectioners' sugar into ½ cup peanut butter. Beat 2 egg whites until stiff and fold into first mixture. Drop from teaspoon on foil-covered sheet and bake in 375°F. oven 10 minutes. Makes 18.

SWEDISH ALMOND WAFERS
(Mandelran)

½ cup butter
½ cup sugar
2 eggs, beaten
½ teaspoon vanilla

1⅓ cups all-purpose
flour (instant type
can be used)
½ cup blanched,
chopped or
shredded almonds

Cream butter. Gradually add sugar, beating thoroughly. Add beaten eggs, vanilla and sifted flour. Drop by rounded teaspoonfuls on cookie sheet. Spread in a circular shape. Sprinkle with almonds and bake in moderate oven (350°F.) 12 to 15 minutes. Remove from pan and while still hot, shape cookies over a rolling pin. Makes about 3 dozen.

ALMOND-COCONUT MERINGUE DROPS

3 egg whites
⅔ cup sugar
3 tablespoons flour
¼ teaspoon salt
1½ cups packaged
grated coconut

½ cup finely chopped
almonds
½ teaspoon each
vanilla and almond
extracts

Beat egg whites until frothy. Gradually add sugar, beating until stiff. Carefully fold in remaining ingredients. Drop by teaspoonfuls onto greased cookie sheet and bake in slow oven (325°F.) about 15 minutes. Makes about 3 dozen.

TOASTED FILBERT KISSES

Beat 3 egg whites to soft, moist peaks; gradually beat in 1 cup sugar and ⅛ teaspoon salt. Continue beating until mixture is thick and glossy and egg white will stand in peaks. Fold in 1 teaspoon grated lemon rind, ½ teaspoon cinnamon and 1 cup toasted and ground filberts. Drop from teaspoon on buttered cookie sheets. Bake in slow oven (275°F.) 20 to 25 minutes. **Can be frozen.** Makes 72. **To toast filberts:** Spread nuts in shallow baking pan containing 1 teaspoon melted butter. Brown in hot oven (400°F.), stirring every 5 minutes. Turn out on brown paper to cool.

GINGERBREAD COOKIES
Easy to cut in two basic shapes and decorate to your heart's delight. Page 90

plate 1

EASY BAR COOKIES

Back row, left to right: Lemon Squares p. 29, Chocolate-Chip Coconut
Bars p. 23, Double-Peanut Bars p. 35, Cocoa-Graham Bars p. 20,
Coffee-Nut Bars p. 34, Superfudgy Saucepan Brownies p. 16,

plate 2

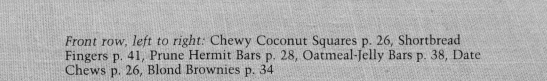

Front row, left to right: Chewy Coconut Squares p. 26, Shortbread Fingers p. 41, Prune Hermit Bars p. 28, Oatmeal-Jelly Bars p. 38, Date Chews p. 26, Blond Brownies p. 34

plate 3

COOKIES FOR
PARTIES
AND SPECIAL
OCCASIONS

plate 4

Left to right, top row: Almond Tarts, filled and unfilled p. 142,
Nut Squares p. 31,
Middle row: Jam Diagonals p. 136, Cereal-Date Wreaths p. 145, Apricot
Turnovers p. 98, Pepper-and-Spice Cookies p. 149
Bottom Row: Walnut Crescents p. 139, Nutmeg Rounds p. 113, Cocoa Logs
p. 129, Marbled Cookies p. 107

plate 5

OATMEAL COOKIES

Clockwise from Top: Trailside Oatmeal Treats p. 48, Coconut Crisps p. 45, Oatmeal-Lemonade Bars p. 38, Raw-Apple Cookies p. 58, All-American Oatmeal Crisps p. 44, Grandma's Favorite Oatmeal Cookies p. 46, Double-Treat Walnut Cookies p. 48, No-Bake Oatmeal Dandies p. 37

plate 6

plate 7

FUDGY
OATMEAL
SQUARES
Page 21

plate 8

MRS. JANSSEN'S PECAN DROPS

½ cup butter or
  margarine, softened
⅔ cup sugar
1 egg yolk
½ teaspoon vanilla

⅛ teaspoon cream of
  tartar
1 cup flour
⅓ cup finely chopped
  pecans
Pecan halves

In large bowl of mixer cream butter and sugar. Add egg yolk and vanilla: beat until mixture is light and fluffy. Beat in cream of tartar. Stir in flour and chopped pecans. Drop by heaping ½ teaspoonfuls 1 inch apart on lightly greased cookie sheet. Press pecan half onto center of each. Bake in preheated 300°F. oven until rich golden, 23 to 25 minutes. Remove at once to wire racks; cool. Makes 48 to 60.

SESAME WAFERS

With their distinctive nutty flavor, these are satisfying to anyone who loves nutmeats. For variety, substitute one cup finely ground nuts for sesame seeds.

1½ cups light brown
  sugar, packed
¾ cup melted butter
1 egg
1 teaspoon vanilla

1 cup toasted sesame
  seeds
1¼ cups sifted flour
¼ teaspoon baking
  powder
¼ teaspoon salt

Mix sugar, butter, egg, and vanilla. Stir in seeds, flour, baking powder and salt. Drop by half teaspoonfuls on buttered cookie sheets; allow for spreading. Bake in moderate oven (375°F.) 10 minutes. Remove from pans at once. Store wafers airtight. Can be frozen. Makes 60.

Spicy Fruit and Nut Cookies

JAMAICAN COCONUT COOKIES

Recreate the spicy scent of a palm-fringed island with these cookies.

¼ cup butter
1 cup sugar
2 cups flaked coconut
2 eggs, beaten
1½ cups sifted flour

½ teaspoon salt
3 teaspoons baking
  powder
1 teaspoon allspice
½ teaspoon ginger

Cream butter and sugar thoroughly. Add coconut and eggs; mix well. Sift flour with remaining ingredients; gradually stir into the coconut mixture. Drop 1 teaspoon at a time onto greased cookie sheet. Bake in hot oven (400°F.) 8 to 10 minutes, or until well browned around the edges. Cool. Store airtight. Makes 5 dozen.

ORANGE-SPICE COOKIES

Easy drop cookies with cakelike texture.

1¼ cups flour
1 teaspoon ginger
¼ teaspoon ground
  cloves
½ teaspoon baking
  soda
⅛ teaspoon salt
½ cup butter or
  margarine, softened

½ cup packed brown
  sugar
2 tablespoons
  molasses
1 egg
½ cup chopped nuts
Grated peel of 1
  orange

Stir together flour, ginger, cloves, baking soda and salt; set aside. In large bowl of mixer cream butter, sugar and molasses. Add egg, nuts and orange peel and beat well. Gradually stir in flour mixture until blended. Drop by rounded teaspoonfuls 2 inches apart on lightly greased cookie sheet. Bake in preheated 350°F. oven 12 minutes or until light brown. Remove to rack to cool. Makes about 42.

SCOTCH ROCKS

Hard cookies with raisins, nuts, spices and coffee.

3 cups sifted flour
½ teaspoon ground cinnamon
1 teaspoon each mace, nutmeg, allspice and baking soda
2 cups chopped raisins
1 cup soft butter or margarine
1¾ cups light-brown sugar, packed
3 eggs, beaten
1½ teaspoons vanilla
1 teaspoon rose water (optional)
2 tablespoons cold, strong coffee
1½ cups chopped nuts

Sift 2¾ cups flour with spices and baking soda. Dredge raisins with remaining ¼ cup flour. Cream butter and sugar until light. Add eggs, flavorings, raisins and nuts. Add flour, working until raisins and nuts are well distributed through the dough. Drop by teaspoonfuls on greased cookie sheets. Bake in moderate oven (350°F.) until slightly browned, about 15 minutes. Makes about 7½ dozen cookies.

LIZZIES

These cookies improve with a few weeks' aging in tightly closed jar.

1½ cups raisins
¼ cup bourbon or orange juice
2 tablespoons butter or margarine
¼ cup packed light-brown sugar
1 egg
¾ cup flour
¾ teaspoon baking soda
¾ teaspoon cinnamon
¼ teaspoon nutmeg
¼ teaspoon ground cloves
½ pound (2 cups) pecan halves or broken walnut halves
¼ pound citron, diced
½ pound candied cherries
Confectioners' sugar (optional)

Stir together raisins and bourbon; let stand 1 hour. Cream butter until fluffy; beat in brown sugar; beat in egg. Mix flour, baking soda and spices; add to creamed mixture and stir well. Add raisin-bourbon mixture, pecans and fruits; mix well. Drop by teaspoonfuls about 1 inch apart on greased cookie sheets. Bake in preheated 325°F. oven about 15 minutes. Remove cookies at once to cool on racks. Before serving, sprinkle with confectioners' sugar. Store airtight in cool dry place. Can be frozen. Makes about 60. **NOTE:** Recipe can be doubled.

SWEDISH CHRISTMAS FRUIT COOKIES
(Julfruktkakor)

¾ cup butter or margarine
1 cup packed dark-brown sugar
1 cup granulated sugar
2 eggs, beaten
1 teaspoon baking soda
½ cup dairy sour cream
3½ cups all-purpose flour (instant type can be used)

¼ cup potato flour or cornstarch
1 teaspoon salt
1 teaspoon vanilla
1 cup chopped raisins
½ cup cut-up candied orange or lemon peel
1 cup cut-up candied cherries
1 cup chopped nuts

Cream butter and add sugars and eggs. Dissolve baking soda in sour cream and add. Mix flour, potato flour and salt and add half to first mixture. Add vanilla, fruit and nuts and mix thoroughly. Add remaining dry ingredients. Drop by teaspoonfuls or shape in small balls and put on greased cookie sheet. Bake in moderate oven (375°F.) about 12 minutes. Makes about 6 dozen.

CONNECTICUT NUTMEG HERMITS

Irregularly shaped cakelike cookies with crisp exteriors.

1¾ cups flour
½ teaspoon nutmeg
½ teaspoon baking soda
¼ teaspoon salt
½ cup butter or margarine, softened

¾ cup packed light-brown sugar
2 eggs
¾ cup raisins
1 cup coarsely chopped walnuts

Stir together flour, nutmeg, baking soda and salt; set aside. In large bowl of mixer cream butter and sugar until fluffy. Beat in eggs one at a time. Stir in flour mixture, raisins and walnuts until well blended. Drop by rounded teaspoonfuls 2 inches apart on ungreased cookie sheets. Bake in preheated 375°F. oven 8 to 10 minutes or until browned and semifirm to touch. Remove to racks to cool. Makes about 36.

GLAZED MINCEMEAT MOUNDS

These unusual drop cookies are very similar to hermits but stay fresh much longer. Store airtight. They are excellent for shipping long distances and for Christmas gift boxes. Can be frozen.

1 cup all-purpose flour (do not use instant type)

¼ teaspoon each salt, baking soda and nutmeg

½ teaspoon cinnamon

½ cup coarsely chopped pecans

⅓ cup softened (not runny or whipped) butter or margarine

⅓ cup packed dark-brown sugar

1 egg

½ cup mincemeat (prepared by recipe below)

1 tablespoon dairy sour cream or buttermilk

Mix dry ingredients, add nuts and set aside. Cream butter and sugar, using an electric mixer, if available. Add egg. Combine mixtures, add mincemeat and sour cream, and mix by hand. Drop batter by heaping teaspoonfuls to form mounds on cookie sheet, leaving 2 inches between mounds. Bake in hot oven (400°F.) 10 to 12 minutes, or until the cookies are done in the middle; break one open to see. Remove from oven, and while cookies are still hot, spread each with glaze. Loosen mounds from pan with a pancake turner. Makes about 2 dozen.

Vanilla Glaze In a mixing bowl, place 1½ cups confectioners' sugar, a dash of salt, 1 teaspoon vanilla, 2 tablespoons melted butter or margarine and 2 tablespoons cream or evaporated milk (or enough to make a smooth paste) and stir briskly. Prepare this while the cookies bake. Glaze can be stored in a jar with a tight-fitting lid and refrigerated a few hours before using, if desired.

Home Touches for Bought Mincemeat To each 2 cups of bought mincemeat add: 1/2 cup shredded peeled apple, 1 teaspoon (or more to taste) mixed spices (especially cinnamon, nutmeg and coriander), 2 tablespoons diced citron, 2 tablespoons diced candied orange peel, 2 tablespoons diced candied lemon peel, 2 teaspoons orange juice, 1 teaspoon lemon juice, 2 tablespoons whiskey or brandy, 1 to 2 tablespoons (to taste) rum or sherry. Mix well, cover and let stand at least 24 hours before using. **Note:** Any kind of bought mincemeat can be used. Prepare packaged mincemeat as directed before measuring.

RAISIN NUGGETS

1½ cups flour
2 teaspoons baking
    powder
1 teaspoon cinnamon
½ teaspoon salt
¾ cup butter or
    margarine, softened

1 cup packed brown
    sugar
2 eggs
1 cup chopped nuts
1 cup raisins

Stir flour, baking powder, cinnamon and salt together; set aside. Cream butter and sugar until light. Beat in eggs one at a time until well blended. Stir flour mixture into egg mixture with nuts and raisins until well blended. Drop by teaspoonfuls on greased cookie sheets and bake in preheated 350°F. oven until lightly browned, about 12 minutes. Remove to rack to cool. Makes about 4 dozen.

Plain and Sugary Drop Cookies

GLACÉ LACE COOKIES

This cookie is a cross between candy and cake. The thin brittle wafers keep a long time. They make fine gifts but are too fragile to ship.

½ cup softened (not runny or whipped) butter
2 cups packed dark-brown sugar

2 eggs
¾ cup all-purpose flour (instant type can be used)

2 teaspoons double-acting baking powder
½ teaspoon salt

Cream butter with sugar, using fingers. Beat in eggs, one at a time, then stir in flour, baking powder and salt. Spread foil on cookie sheets and butter lightly. Drop dough onto foil by measuring half-teaspoonfuls 2 inches apart (do not flatten; cookies spread while baking). Bake in hot oven (400°F.) 4 to 5 minutes, or until cookies are caramel-brown. When cookies seem done, remove from oven and lift one with pancake turner. If cookies stick to foil, put back in oven. Do not try to remove cookies while hot. Place at once in refrigerator and chill 5 minutes, or until thoroughly cooled, then peel off from foil. Use foil again and again until all dough has been used. (It is not necessary to butter foil after first time.) Keep two pans going at once, putting one in the oven as soon as the other is removed. Makes about 18 dozen.

Variation 2 cups finely chopped pecans can be added to the flour and then blended with the fingers into the butter-egg mixture. Bake as directed. Makes about 14 dozen. (Nuts make the cookies a little thicker.)

SOUR-CREAM DROP COOKIES

These taste like rich pound cake.

1 cup soft butter or margarine
Sugar
2 eggs
3½ cups unsifted flour
½ teaspoon baking soda

½ teaspoon salt
1 teaspoon nutmeg
¼ cup soured heavy cream
Raisins or nut halves

Cream butter and 1½ cups sugar until light. Add eggs and beat well. Add sifted dry ingredients and soured cream; mix well. Drop by teaspoonfuls on cookie sheets. Put a raisin or nut in the center of each. Sprinkle with sugar. Bake in moderate oven (350°F.) about 12 minutes. Makes about 7 dozen.

BROWN-EDGE SUGAR COOKIES

A sampling of the kind of basic, simply delicious drop cookies that have appeared in Woman's Day *over the years.*

½ cup butter or margarine	1¼ cups all-purpose flour
¾ cup sugar	¼ teaspoon salt
1 egg	¼ teaspoon double-
½ teaspoon vanilla	acting baking
2 tablespoons milk	powder

Cream butter until light and fluffy, then beat in sugar and continue creaming. Beat in egg and vanilla. Stir in milk, then add flour mixed with salt and baking powder and mix well. Drop by teaspoonfuls onto greased cookie sheets about 2 inches apart. Bake in preheated 350°F. oven 10 minutes, or until edges are lightly browned. Remove at once to rack to cool. Makes about 3 dozen.

BRANDY WAFERS

A lacy, crisp cookie, rolled up after baking.

½ cup unsulfured molasses	¼ teaspoon salt
½ cup butter, softened	⅔ cup sugar
1¼ cups sifted cake flour	1 tablespoon ground ginger
	3 tablespoons brandy

Preheat oven to slow (300°F.). In saucepan, heat molasses to boiling. Add butter and stir until melted. Mix next 4 ingredients and add gradually, stirring. Add brandy and stir until well mixed. Drop by measuring half-teaspoonfuls 3 inches apart on greased cookie sheet, baking 6 at a time. Bake about 10 minutes. Cool 1 minute, then remove with spatula and roll at once around handle of wooden spoon. (If removed too soon, wafer will shrink together; if not soon enough, wafer will be too brittle to roll. If too brittle, put back in oven a few minutes to soften.) Repeat until all of mixture is used, lightly greasing cookie sheet each time with paper towel, thus removing any crumbs. Makes about 7 dozen.

To Store Store airtight. Can be frozen. Good keepers if kept in cool place. Not good shippers; cookies break easily.

V
ROLLED COOKIES

No other type of cookie is quite as appealing to children as rolled cookies. And at Christmastime, there is nothing more fun or exciting for *all* ages than seeing these cookies come out of the oven, ready for hanging on the tree.

The basic technique is simple. First the dough is mixed and chilled at least an hour, preferably more. Then it is rolled out into a flat sheet (using about as much dough per batch as for a pie crust) and cut with tin or plastic cookie cutters. The cookies are then transferred one at a time onto sheets to bake.

The less handling and flouring of the dough, the more tender the cookies will be. One of the ways to avoid sticky dough is to allow a long chilling in the icebox, preferably overnight. Another is to use a pastry cloth and rolling pin.

Roll the dough from the center out, to about one-eighth-inch thickness unless otherwise specified. With each pass over the dough, pick up the roller rather than pushing it back and forth. This helps to avoid stretching and toughening.

Placement of the cutters on the dough is important. Start at one end and cut the cookies as close together as possible, keeping dough scraps to a minimum.

Use flat, greased cookie sheets; pans with rims make it difficult to remove cookies.

A thin, flexible spatula makes easiest the transfer of cookies onto and off of the sheets.

Push the scraps together and reroll them, taking care not to incorporate too much extra flour into the dough.

Work only with one piece of dough at a time, keeping the remaining portions chilled until you are ready to use them.

Cutters are fun to collect. Keep them clean and keep the edges smooth. Store cutters in a dry place where they will stay rust-free; with every generation of use, their sentimental value increases.

If sticking becomes a problem, flour the edges of the cutter between each use.

Some cutters are too intricate for certain dough, and the design is lost in the baking. If you suspect this might be the case, cut a sample and bake it to be sure the shape holds up.

Cutters are not necessary for making rolled cookies. The easiest cutting method—and the one that avoids having to reroll scraps—is simply to use a knife and cut squares, diamonds or rectangles from the rolled dough.

A traditional way to make your own cutting patterns (to use once and then discard) is to draw a pattern on cardboard, cut it out, lay it gently on the dough and cut around the shape with a knife. Work quickly to avoid dampening the cardboard and transferring its taste to the dough.

Sugar and Butter Cookies

SUGAR COOKIES

A basic recipe—to use with cutters or without.

5 cups all-purpose flour
2 cups sugar
1 teaspoon baking soda
1 teaspoon baking powder

½ teaspoon salt
¼ teaspoon nutmeg
1 cup butter, or part butter and part margarine

3 eggs
½ cup buttermilk
1 teaspoon vanilla
Cinnamon or nutmeg sugar

Sift flour with 1 cup sugar and next 4 ingredients into large bowl. Cut in butter with pastry blender or, in the good old-fashioned way, with fingers, until crumbly. Beat eggs slightly and add remaining sugar gradually, beating in thoroughly. Blend in buttermilk and vanilla and add to crumb base. Blend well, chill until ready to bake or proceed with rolling and shaping at once. Turn out about a quarter of the dough onto lightly floured board or pastry cloth and roll about ⅛ inch thick for an average cookie or ¼ inch thick for a more substantial cookie. Cut as desired, dip each cookie top lightly into mixture of granulated sugar spiced with cinnamon or nutmeg (about ¼ teaspoon spice to ½ cup sugar) and place cookie on lightly greased cookie sheet. Bake in moderate oven (375°F.) 8 to 15 minutes, depending on thickness, or until lightly browned and firm to the touch. Transfer to wire racks to cool. Continue with remaining dough. Or roll dough into rectangular sheet, dust top with sugar-spice mixture and cut with tip of sharp knife or pizza wheel in shapes such as slender fingers, squares or diamonds. Proceed as above. Makes 6 to 8 dozen.

SWEDISH CHOCOLATE BUTTER COOKIES
(Choklad Mördegskakor)

½ cup butter, melted and cooled
½ cup sugar
1 egg, beaten
1 teaspoon vanilla

2 cups all-purpose flour (instant type can be used)
1 teaspoon baking powder

2 tablespoons cocoa
1 egg white, slightly beaten
Chopped blanched almonds

Combine butter, ½ cup sugar and egg and beat thoroughly. Add vanilla. Add flour sifted with baking powder and cocoa. Chill. Roll out quite thin and cut in bell or other Christmas shapes. Brush tops with slightly beaten egg white and sprinkle with sugar and almonds. Put on greased cookie sheet and bake in moderate oven (375°F.) 5 minutes. Makes about 4 dozen.

BUTTER THINS

½ cup butter, slightly
   softened
½ cup sugar
1½ cups unsifted all-
   purpose flour
½ teaspoon cream of
   tartar

¼ teaspoon baking
   soda
Dash of nutmeg
1 egg
½ teaspoon vanilla

Working with hands, cream butter and sugar until blended. Work in dry ingredients until smooth, then add egg and vanilla and mix well. Wrap in plastic and chill 2 hours, or until firm enough to roll. Roll a small amount at a time on lightly floured surface until very thin. Cut in rounds with floured 2-inch cutter and put on ungreased baking sheet. Bake in slow oven (300°F.) 12 minutes, or until lightly browned. Remove to racks to cool. Makes 50 to 60 cookies.

COCONUT SUGAR COOKIES

A thin, crisp cookie that you form with a cookie cutter.

⅔ cup butter or
   margarine
⅔ cup sugar
2 eggs
1 teaspoon vanilla
2 cups sifted flour
1½ teaspoons baking
   powder

½ teaspoon salt
1 cup flaked coconut,
   chopped
Colored Vanilla
   Frosting (see below)

Cream butter and sugar. Beat in eggs, one at a time; add vanilla. Sift flour with baking powder and salt and stir in gradually, blending thoroughly. Add coconut. Chill until firm enough to roll. Roll out dough to ⅛-inch thickness on floured board. Cut with floured bell or other cookie cutter. Bake on ungreased cookie sheet in moderate oven (375°F.) 12 minutes, or until golden brown. Cool and decorate with Vanilla Frosting, tinted as desired with food coloring. Makes about 4 dozen 1½-inch cookies.

Vanilla Frosting

Beat until smooth: 1½ cups sifted confectioners' sugar, 2 tablespoons cream and 1½ teaspoons vanilla. To color, add a few drops of vegetable food coloring.

DANISH SAND COOKIES
(Sandkager)

½ cup butter
Sugar
1 egg, beaten
1¾ cups all-purpose
 flour
¼ cup cornstarch

2 teaspoons baking
 powder
1 egg white
Blanched almonds
½ teaspoon cinnamon

Cream butter, gradually add 1 cup sugar, then the egg. Mix flour, cornstarch and baking powder. Add to creamed mixture, blending thoroughly. Chill. Roll thin on floured board and cut with 2½-inch doughnut cutter. Brush with egg white. Split almonds and arrange 3 halves on each cookie at equal distances. Sprinkle with mixture of 2 tablespoons sugar and the cinnamon. Put on a greased cookie sheet and bake in moderate oven (350°F.) 8 to 10 minutes. Makes about 5 dozen.

ICE CREAM COOKIES

In the Gay Nineties ladies gathered in ice cream parlors in midafternoon for a soda or sundae, usually accompanied by these cookies.

½ cup butter,
 softened
⅓ cup sugar
1 teaspoon vanilla

¼ teaspoon salt
1 egg
1¼ cups all-purpose
 flour

Cream butter and sugar until light. Add vanilla, salt and egg and beat well. Add flour and mix with fingers until ingredients hold together. If too soft to roll, chill until firm. On floured board with floured rolling pin, roll half the dough at a time very thin. Cut with round 2½-inch cutter and put on ungreased cookie sheet. Bake in moderate oven (350°F.) 8 minutes, or until edges are browned. Remove from sheets to cake racks. Let stand until cold, then store airtight. Makes about 4 dozen.

EDINBURGH SHORTBREAD

*Shortbread, Scotland's prize cookie, is popular not only in its
homeland but throughout the British Commonwealth. It is always
served in Scotland for Christmas and Hogmanay, or New Year's Eve.
The first footers, or the first callers to put their feet across the threshold
of a house after the new year is born, expect a bit of shortbread
as part of the welcome ceremony. It makes a superb Christmas gift.*

2½ cups all-purpose flour	1 cup butter, at room temperature
¼ teaspoon salt	1 tablespoon vanilla or almond extract, or half of each
1 cup sugar	

Mix dry ingredients. Add butter and flavoring and mix with fingers until
mixture forms a paste that holds together. With floured rolling pin, on lightly
floured board or marble table or slab, roll dough to ½-inch thickness. (If too soft
to roll, chill about 30 minutes in uncovered bowl. If dough is too crumbly to
hold together, add 1 or more tablespoons milk.) Cut in fancy shapes with floured
cutters, put 1 inch or more apart on cookie sheet and bake in moderate oven
(375°F.) 10 minutes, or until lightly browned on top. Loosen from pan while hot
and cool on rack. Makes about 30. **NOTE:** Shortbread freezes well.

Ginger Shortbread Prepare shortbread dough, flavoring with 1 teaspoon vanilla
and 1 teaspoon ground ginger. Roll ¼ inch thick and cut with 2-inch round or
fancy cutter. Bake 8 to 10 minutes and cool. Spread thinly with following
frosting: Mix 1½ cups confectioners' sugar, 1 teaspoon ginger or ¼ cup minced
candied ginger, 2 tablespoons soft butter and 1 to 3 tablespoons milk. Frosting
can be tinted pale yellow or green.

Molded Shortbread Buy small tin candy molds. Press uncooked shortbread dough
into each mold with fingers, then even tops with dull knife. Set molds on flat
cookie pan, dough side up. Bake as directed in basic recipe. (Time will depend
on size of molds.) Remove from oven and let remain in molds until cooled to
room temperature. To remove, tap bottom of each mold with handle of knife. A
box of these makes a nice Christmas gift. Be sure to pack airtight.

Petticoat Tails These are merely shortbread cut a different way. Some say Mary,
Queen of Scots, brought the recipe to her native Scotland from France and that
the term "petticoat tails" was a corruption of *petits gâteaux*—little cakes.
Others insist that these cookies got their name because they were the shape of
the petticoats worn in the sixteenth century when the cookies were originated.
But no matter, they are delicious anyway. To shape the Petticoat Tails, roll
shortbread dough ½ inch thick, put an 8-inch dessert plate on dough and cut
around it with a floured pastry wheel or dull knife. With a 2½- to 3-inch round

cookie cutter, remove center of disk. Then cut remainder in wedges, 8 to 12 to each disk. Put on cookie sheet and bake as in basic recipe. **NOTE:** If desired, brush unbaked shortbread with 1 egg white mixed with 1 tablespoon water. Dust with colored decorating sugar and bake as directed.

Pitcaithly Bannocks Prepare shortbread dough, adding ⅔ cup coarsely chopped toasted blanched almonds and 2 tablespoons finely chopped candied orange peel to dry ingredients. Flavor with half orange and half almond extracts.

Shortbread Surprises Roll a teaspoon or more of dough between floured palms to form a 1-inch ball. Insert one third of a date, half a pecan or almond, a candied cherry, small round gumdrop, a sliver of candied ginger or other candied fruit, leaving fruit or nut exposed or working into center of ball and rerolling to smooth it. Bake 8 to 10 minutes. Cooled cookie balls can be dipped in different colored and flavored frostings or put on waxed paper and spread with frosting. Sprinkle with cookie coconut, chopped nuts or chocolate shot while frosting is still soft, if desired. For Christmas boxes sprinkle frosting with tiny dragées, colored sugar or multicolored candies.

LEMON SUGAR COOKIES

Make dough ahead and chill overnight.

1 cup butter or margarine, softened	3 tablespoons lemon juice
1 cup sugar	4 cups flour
1 teaspoon vanilla	1 tablespoon water
½ teaspoon salt	Colored sugar or chopped nuts
1 whole egg	
1 egg, separated	

Cream butter, sugar, vanilla and salt until fluffy. Beat in whole egg, egg yolk and lemon juice. Stir in flour until well blended. Divide dough in fourths and wrap each airtight; chill overnight. On lightly floured surface roll out each ⅛-inch thick. With floured small holiday cookie or doughnut cutters cut in desired shapes (reroll scraps). Place ½ inch apart on lightly greased cookie sheets. Brush with egg white slightly beaten with water; sprinkle with sugar. Bake in preheated 350°F. oven until golden, 8 to 10 minutes. Cool on racks. Store airtight in cool dry place. Makes 96 to 120.

SWISS CRISPS

These magnificent sugar cookies have a subtle flavor and a truly continental appeal. Serve them for your most elegant parties. They also make a welcome Christmas gift but are too fragile to ship. Cut recipe in half to make a smaller amount.

1 cup softened (not runny or whipped) butter
Sugar
1 egg yolk
1 tablespoon grated semi-sweet chocolate
¼ teaspoon salt
1¼ teaspoons cinnamon

1½ tablespoons Grand Marnier or Cointreau
2½ cups all-purpose flour (do not use instant type)
½ teaspoon baking powder
Finely chopped almonds (optional)

Cream butter and 1 cup sugar, using electric mixer, if available. Add egg yolk, chocolate, salt and ¼ teaspoon cinnamon. Add liqueur, flour and baking powder. Mix with hands until dough holds together. This is a soft dough, so chill until firm enough to roll. Roll very thin, using a small amount of dough at a time. Cut into fancy shapes. Transfer to cookie sheet, allowing ½ inch between cookies. Sprinkle with a mixture of 2 tablespoons sugar and remaining cinnamon or with almonds. Bake in moderate oven (350°F.) 10 to 12 minutes, or until lightly browned. Loosen at once with a pancake turner and let stand until cool. Store airtight. These cookies make fine escorts for ice cream or mousse, cut-up fruit, parfaits or any other dessert. Makes about 12 dozen small cookies.

Nut Cookies
NUT RIBBON COOKIES

Use filberts, walnuts or pecans.

1 cup soft butter or margarine
½ cup granulated sugar
1 teaspoon almond extract
1 egg
2 cups unsifted all-purpose flour

2 teaspoons baking powder
¼ teaspoon salt
½ cup chopped nuts (filberts, walnuts or pecans)
Confectioners' sugar

Cream butter, sugar and almond extract until light and fluffy. Add egg and beat well. Sift flour, baking powder and salt and add. Mix well. Chill about 45 minutes. On floured board, roll dough to a rectangle ¼ inch thick. Sprinkle with nuts and press in lightly with rolling pin. With fluted pastry cutter, dipped in flour, cut dough in strips 1 inch wide by 2½ inches long. Put on greased cookie sheet and press tops lightly with floured tines of fork. Bake in hot oven (425° F.) 5 or 6 minutes. Remove and cool. Dust with confectioners' sugar. Makes about 5 dozen.

NORWEGIAN ROYAL FANS
(Kongevifter)

1 cup sweet butter
1 cup sugar
4 eggs
½ cup coarsely chopped blanched almonds
1 teaspoon almond extract

1 teaspoon baking powder
3¼ cups all purpose flour (instant type can be used)
Finely chopped almonds

Cream butter and sugar until light. Add 3 unbeaten eggs, one at a time, beating well after each addition. Add coarsely chopped nuts and almond extract. Sift baking powder with flour and add to mixture. Chill. Roll out on floured board to a rectangle ⅛ inch thick. Cut in 3½-inch-wide strips, then in 3½-inch triangles. Put on greased cookie sheet or pan, brush with remaining egg, beaten, and sprinkle with finely chopped nuts. Bake in moderate oven (375° F.) about 8 minutes. Makes about 4 dozen.

PEANUT WHIRLS

A crisp pinwheel cookie.

½ cup vegetable
    shortening
½ cup smooth peanut
    butter
1 cup sugar
1 egg
1 teaspoon vanilla

1¼ cups sifted flour
½ teaspoon baking
    soda
½ teaspoon salt
2 tablespoons milk
1 package (6 ounces)
    semisweet
    chocolate pieces,
    melted and cooled

Cream shortening, peanut butter and sugar until light. Beat in egg and vanilla. Add sifted dry ingredients and milk. Chill until firm enough to roll. Turn out on lightly floured board or cloth and roll into a rectangle 14 × 11 inches. Spread with chocolate, roll as for jelly roll and chill ½ hour. Cut in ¼-inch slices and put on cookie sheets. Bake in moderate oven (350° F.) about 10 minutes. Makes about 3½ dozen.

Note: If necessary to chill dough longer than ½ hour, warm up slightly before slicing as chocolate becomes brittle if chilled too long.

SWISS BASLER BRUNSLI

Named for the Swiss city of Basle.

1 cup sugar
1 cup ground
    almonds
½ cup grated
    unsweetened
    chocolate

2 tablespoons kirsch
1 teaspoon cinnamon
¼ teaspoon cloves
2 egg whites

Combine all ingredients except egg whites. Beat whites until almost stiff. Add the almond-chocolate mixture and work all together to form a dough. Roll or pat to about 1-inch thickness on a board lightly sprinkled with sugar, and cut in rosettes (the traditional shape) or in 1½-inch circles. Put on greased sheet; let dry 2 or 3 hours. Bake in 325°F. oven 10 to 15 minutes. Makes 18.

DANISH THIN ALMOND COOKIES
(Tynde Mandelkager)

½ cup butter or
  margarine
1 cup packed dark-
  brown sugar
1 egg, beaten
½ teaspoon vanilla
½ teaspoon almond
  extract
1½ cups all-purpose
  flour (instant type
  can be used)

¼ cup potato flour or
  cornstarch
1 teaspoon baking
  powder
½ teaspoon salt
½ cup blanched
  almonds, ground

Cream butter and add sugar gradually, blending thoroughly. Add egg, vanilla and almond extracts. Mix dry ingredients and add to creamed mixture. Add almonds. Chill dough overnight. Roll out very thin on a floured board and cut with fancy cutters. Put on cookie sheet and bake in moderate oven (350°F.) about 5 minutes. Makes about 5 dozen.

ITALIAN MUSCATELS

½ cup plus ½
  teaspoon butter
1 cup unblanched
  almonds
1 cup sugar
2 tablespoons dried
  grated orange peel
1½ cups sifted flour

1½ teaspoons baking
  powder
1½ teaspoons
  cinnamon
1½ teaspoons allspice
½ cup muscatel wine
Frosting (see below)
Colored sugar

Melt ½ teaspoon butter in skillet; add almonds and brown over low heat. Cool. Chop. Cream ½ cup butter; gradually beat in sugar; add orange peel and almonds. Sift flour with baking powder and spices; add alternately with wine to butter mixture. Chill 1 hour. Turn out on sugared board; pat or roll gently to ⅓-inch thickness. Cut with 1½-inch scalloped cookie cutter; put on buttered cookie sheets. Bake in moderate oven (350°F.) 12 to 15 minutes. While hot, frost and sprinkle with colored sugar. Can be frozen. Makes 96. **Frosting:** Add 1 teaspoon lemon juice to 2 unbeaten egg whites; stir in confectioners' sugar until of spreading consistency.

FRENCH PRALINE FINGERS

Chewy almond cookies—good with ice cream. There is no flour in this recipe.

Confectioners' sugar
¼ cup unblanched almonds
1 cup blanched almonds, finely ground in blender

1 egg white, slightly beaten
Candied orange peel or candied fruits
White decorating frosting (optional)

To make praline, put ¼ cup confectioners' sugar and unblanched almonds in small heavy skillet and cook, stirring, over medium heat until sugar dissolves and almonds are lightly browned and coated with sugar. Pour onto cookie sheet to cool. When hard, break in small pieces and grind fine in blender (about the texture of cornmeal). In mixing bowl, combine praline with 1 cup confectioners' sugar and next 2 ingredients, mix well, then gather particles in ball with hands. Dust board lightly with confectioners' sugar. Divide dough in half, then divide each half in 4 equal pieces. Shape each piece in 10-inch long roll. Put rolls parallel to each other and cut crosswise in 2-inch pieces. Put on well-greased cookie sheets and decorate each with a piece or strip of orange peel. Bake in preheated 325°F. oven 10 to 12 minutes. Let stand 2 minutes, then remove to racks to cool. Decorate with white frosting, if desired. Store airtight at room temperature. Makes 40.

Note: A slice of raw apple in airtight container will keep cookies chewy.

SERBIAN WALNUT-STRIPS

Mix 1 pound walnuts, ground, and 1 cup granulated sugar. Add 1 teaspoon lemon juice and 3 unbeaten egg whites; knead until mixture sticks together. Pat out on sugared board to a rectangle 3 inches wide and ½ inch thick. Beat 1 egg white stiff; gradually beat in ¾ cup confectioners' sugar. Spread over walnut mixture. Cut in 1½ × ¾-inch strips. Arrange cookies in rows on well-buttered cookie sheets. Bake in very slow oven (200° F.) 20 minutes. Store airtight. Makes 72.

CHINESE ALMOND COOKIES

1 cup all-purpose
  flour, lightly
  spooned into cup
¼ teaspoon salt
⅓ cup butter
⅓ cup sugar
1 egg, separated
1 tablespoon milk
¼ teaspoon almond
  extract

2 hard-cooked egg
  yolks, sieved
3 tablespoons finely
  chopped
  blanched almonds
Blanched almond
  halves

Mix flour and salt. Cream butter and sugar together until light. Add raw egg yolk and milk and beat well. Add flavoring, sieved hard-cooked egg yolks, flour and salt and stir until well blended. Add chopped almonds and mix well. Chill dough. Roll out ⅛-inch thick on lightly floured board or pastry canvas and cut with 2-¼-inch cookie cutter. Brush tops with slightly beaten egg white and place a blanched almond half in center of each cookie. Bake on greased baking sheet in preheated 325°F. oven 10 to 12 minutes, or until lightly browned. Makes about 2 dozen. Cookies can be made ahead, wrapped in foil and frozen. They keep well at least 3 months. Defrost at room temperature.

Spicy Rolled Cookies

CORIANDER COOKIE THINS

2 cups all-purpose
  flour
1 cup sugar
2 tablespoons ground
  coriander
¾ cup butter or
  margarine

1 egg, slightly beaten
1 teaspoon vanilla
Colored or white
  sugar

Mix first 3 ingredients in bowl. Add butter and cut in with pastry blender. Blend egg and vanilla and work into mixture with hands to form a smooth dough. Roll in ½-inch balls and put on ungreased cookie sheets. Flatten with moistened bottom of measuring cup dipped in sugar. Bake in hot oven (400°F.) 6 to 8 minutes. Makes 7 to 8 dozen.

SPICED ORANGE FLOWERS

These orange, allspice and nutmeg cookies keep well.

1 cup soft butter or
  margarine
1½ cups sugar
1 tablespoon grated
  orange rind
1 egg
3 tablespoons orange
  juice

3 cups sifted flour
1 teaspoon baking
  powder
½ teaspoon salt
½ teaspoon allspice
¾ teaspoon nutmeg
Candied red and
  green cherries

Cream butter and sugar until light. Beat in rind, egg and juice. Add sifted dry ingredients and mix until smooth. Chill if necessary to make stiff enough to roll. Then roll to ⅛-inch thickness and cut with 2-inch diamond-shaped cutter. Put on sheet and bring 2 longest points of each to center, overlapping slightly. Decorate with cherries. Bake in hot oven (400°F.) 8 to 10 minutes. Makes 8 dozen.

CINNAMON BOWKNOTS

2 cups flour
1 tablespoon baking
  powder
1 teaspoon salt
6 tablespoons
  shortening

⅔ cup milk
¼ cup butter or
  margarine, melted
2 tablespoons sugar
  mixed with 1
  teaspoon cinnamon

Combine flour, baking powder and salt in bowl. Cut in shortening until mixture resembles coarse crumbs. Add milk all at once and stir with fork until mixture forms ball and no flour remains. Turn out on lightly floured surface and knead lightly 25 times. Roll out ½ inch thick. Cut with floured 2½-inch doughnut cutter. Twist each ring to form figure 8, place on ungreased cookie sheet and bake in preheated 400°F. oven 12 minutes or until lightly browned. Dip tops in butter, then in sugar-cinnamon mixture. Makes 1 dozen.

CINNAMON CHRISTMAS COOKIES

Cut these into any shape.

½ cup soft butter or
  margarine
Sugar
1 whole egg
2 cups unsifted cake
  flour
1½ teaspoons baking
  powder

¼ teaspoon salt
2 egg whites
½ teaspoon
  cinnamon
Red and green
  sprinkles or finely
  chopped nuts

Cream butter, 1 cup sugar and egg until light. Add sifted flour, baking powder and salt; mix well. Chill overnight. Roll thin on lightly floured board and cut with star or other Christmas cutter. Beat egg whites slightly and brush on cookies. Mix cinnamon and 2 tablespoons sugar. Sprinkle on cookies and add a few colored sprinkles. Bake at 350°F. for about 10 minutes, until lightly browned. Makes about 6 dozen Christmas cookies.

LEMON-CARAWAY COOKIES

A crisp, tasty cookie.

1 egg	½ cup butter or
1 cup sugar	margarine, softened
2 tablespoons lemon	2½ cups all-purpose
juice	flour
2 teaspoons caraway	½ teaspoon baking
seed	soda
	¼ teaspoon salt

In small bowl of electric mixer, beat egg until foamy, then gradually beat in sugar. Add lemon juice, caraway seed and butter and stir just until blended. Gradually stir in flour mixed with baking soda and salt. Shape in 2 rolls about 1-½ inches in diameter, then roll in waxed paper. Chill overnight, or longer if preferred. Slice thin and put on ungreased cookie sheets. Bake in preheated 400°F. oven 7 minutes, or until edges are lightly browned. Remove at once and cool on racks. Makes about 6 dozen.

CHRISTMAS PIGS
(Piparkakut)

Piparkakut, the Christmas pigs of Finland, are typical shapes in other Scandinavian countries too. You can buy pig-shape cookie cutters in Scandinavian gift shops, or make a paper pattern and cut them out with a sharp-tipped knife.

⅔ cup butter or	2 teaspoons each
margarine	ginger and cloves
⅔ cup packed dark-	2 teaspoons baking
brown sugar	soda dissolved in ¼
2 tablespoons dark	cup water
corn syrup or	2½ cups flour
molasses	Confectioners'-sugar
1 tablespoon	icing, homemade
cinnamon	or canned
	(optional)

In medium saucepan stir butter, sugar and corn syrup over low heat until butter is melted. Remove from heat and add cinnamon, ginger and cloves. Cool slightly. Add dissolved baking soda. Add flour and mix until blended. Chill until very firm. Divide dough in eighths and on floured surface roll out each as thin as possible. Cut in pig shapes (reroll scraps); bake on ungreased cookie sheets in preheated 325°F. oven 6 to 8 minutes or until browned. Cool on racks. Decorate pigs with an icing that can be pressed through pastry tube with plain tip. Makes about sixty 4-inch pigs.

SWEDISH GINGER COOKIES
(Pepparkakor)

Small undecorated gingersnaps in any desired shape—hearts, trees, stars, etc.—are baked to be served with coffee on the first Sunday in Advent after the family returns from church and on Lucia Day. Every household has its own special recipe, and the cookies actually seem to improve with age. The heart, of course, is the Swedes' favorite shape for Christmas.

2¼ cups flour	¾ cup sugar
1 teaspoon baking soda	1 small egg
1½ teaspoons each ginger and cinnamon	1 tablespoon light molasses
½ teaspoon cloves	Grated peel and juice (2 tablespoons) of ½ orange
½ cup butter or margarine, softened	Royal Icing (recipe follows)

Stir together flour, soda, ginger, cinnamon and cloves; set aside. In large bowl cream butter and sugar. Add egg and beat until fluffy. Stir in molasses, orange peel and juice; mix well. Stir in flour mixture until blended. Cover and chill until firm enough to roll out, several hours or overnight. Remove small portions of dough at a time from refrigerator and roll out with stockinette-covered rolling pin on lightly floured surface or pastry cloth to slightly less than ⅛-inch thickness. Cut in desired shapes with fancy 2½-inch cookie cutters. Reroll scraps. Place 1 inch apart on lightly greased cookie sheets. Bake in preheated 375°F. oven 8 to 10 minutes or until light brown. (Watch carefully to prevent overbrowning.) Remove from cookie sheets immediately; cool on racks. When cool, outline cookies with Royal Icing, using straight or zigzag lines, swirled loops or dots. (Use decorating tube with ¹⁄₁₆-inch opening, or make a cone out of heavy paper, taping to hold and snipping off tip to make ¹⁄₁₆-inch opening.) Makes about 72.

Royal Icing

1 egg white	¼ teaspoon vanilla
Dash of salt	About 1 cup confectioners' sugar
¼ teaspoon cream of tartar	

In small bowl beat egg white, salt and cream of tartar until stiff peaks form. Add vanilla. Gradually beat in just enough sugar so icing is stiff but still thin enough to push through ¹⁄₁₆-inch decorating tube. Cover icing with damp cloth until ready to use. Makes 1 cup.

GINGERBREAD COOKIES
(shown on plate 1)

With two simple cutters, a person and an animal shape, you can turn out dozens of gingerbread characters for Christmas decorating.

⅔ cup packed light-
  brown sugar
⅔ cup dark corn
  syrup
1 teaspoon ginger
1 teaspoon cinnamon
½ teaspoon ground
  cloves

½ teaspoon salt
1½ teaspoons baking
  soda
⅔ cup butter or
  margarine
1 egg
4 cups flour
Decorating Frosting

Put sugar, syrup, spices and salt in large saucepan (cookies will be mixed in saucepan); bring to boil. Add soda and butter; stir until butter melts. Quickly stir in egg, then add flour; mix well. Chill until firm enough to roll, then roll on lightly floured surface to about ¼-inch thickness. Cut in shapes (see below). Bake on ungreased cookie sheets in preheated 325°F. oven about 15 minutes. Cool on racks. Decorate with frosting, using a pastry tube with a fine point or a paper cone. Makes about 36 five-inch cookies.

DECORATING FROSTING In small bowl of mixer beat 1 egg white with 1 cup plus 2 to 3 tablespoons confectioners' sugar until smooth and of proper consistency to squeeze through pastry tube for decorating (add a little more sugar if necessary).

HOW TO MAKE CUTTERS
If you do not have metal cookie cutters, make your own. Draw your design, keeping it simple and avoiding tiny details that can break off in the baking. Cut a length of stainless-steel strip metal (used to mount antennas to chimneys), bend to match the drawing and shape with long-nosed pliers. Cut off excess metal, leaving overlap of about ½ inch. Secure overlap by gluing with superstrength glue, or roughen surface and use two-part epoxy. (Do not solder, sincer solder has a high lead content.)

LEBKUCHEN FROM NUREMBERG

Christmas wouldn't be Christmas in Germany without lebkuchen and it is an accepted fact that the best lebkuchen come from the little town of Nuremberg. Here's an authentic recipe. They keep well airtight and also freeze and ship well.

1 cup honey
1 egg, well beaten
Grated rind of 1
  lemon
2 tablespoons lemon
  juice
⅔ cup packed dark-
  brown sugar
½ cup almonds,
  slivered or chopped
  fine
½ cup minced citron

2¼ cups all-purpose
  flour (instant type
  can be used)
1 teaspoon cinnamon
½ teaspoon each
  ground cloves,
  allspice, mace,
  freshly grated
  nutmeg, baking
  soda and salt
Glaze
Blanched almonds,
  citron or angelica
  (optional)

Heat the honey just under boiling point in a saucepan. (Use a full-flavored honey such as clover or orange-blossom.) Cool to lukewarm. Add egg, lemon rind, juice and brown sugar. Mix nuts and citron with ¼ cup of flour. Mix remaining flour with spices, baking soda and salt. Combine the honey mixture with dry ingredients. Add the nuts and citron and mix with hands. Put in bowl, cover with foil or waxed paper and set in the refrigerator for 12 or more hours. Divide dough in quarters and roll each into a 6 × 4½-inch rectangle. With pastry wheel, cut each into six 3 × 1½-inch cookies. Place on a buttered cookie sheet about 2 inches apart and spread with glaze. Decorate with halves of blanched almonds and thin slivers of citron or angelica, or leave plain. Put in hot oven (400°F.). Reduce heat at once to 375°F. and bake 15 to 20 minutes, or until cookies just test done. Do not bake until hard and dry; these should be chewy and moist.

GLAZE Beat 1 egg white until stiff. Fold in ⅔ cup confectioners' sugar, dash of salt and ¼ teaspoon vanilla or lemon juice. **NOTE:** Sometimes the cookies are baked without glazing or they are glazed after baking, especially if they are to be decorated for Christmas gifts.

GERMAN PEPPERNUTS
(Pfefferneusse)

Tiny spice cookies that contain pepper as well as several other spices. A drop of brandy on the top before baking causes them to "pop," giving them a characteristic topknot.

3½ cups flour	4 eggs
2 teaspoons cinnamon	2 cups sugar
1 teaspoon baking powder	Grated peel of 1 lemon (1½ teaspoons)
½ teaspoon each nutmeg, allspice and cloves	½ cup finely chopped candied citron
¼ teaspoon each salt, pepper and mace	½ cup unblanched almonds, ground
	3 tablespoons brandy

Stir together flour, cinnamon, baking powder, nutmeg, allspice, cloves, salt, pepper and mace; set aside. In large bowl beat eggs at medium speed of mixer until fluffy. Gradually beat in sugar. Continue beating 15 minutes longer or until thick and fluffy. Add flour mixture in thirds, adding lemon peel, citron and almonds to last third and blending thoroughly after each addition. Turn half the dough out onto lightly floured surface. Roll out ½ inch thick. Cut with 1-inch round cutter (inside of doughnut cutter works well) and place 1 inch apart on greased cookie sheets. Reroll scraps. Let stand uncovered at room temperature overnight. When ready to bake, turn cookies over so moist side is up; put drop of brandy in center of each. Bake in preheated 300°F. oven 20 minutes or until cookies "pop" and are baked through. (Break one in half; if not sticky, it's done.) Remove to racks to cool. Makes 90. **NOTE:** Cookies improve with age. Store in tightly covered container. Add a piece of apple to container a few days before serving to soften them.

SPICY CHOCOLATE STICKS

The spices are cinnamon, cloves and allspice.

4 eggs
2 cups brown sugar,
   packed
1 teaspoon cinnamon
¼ teaspoon allspice
¼ teaspoon cloves
1 package (4 ounces)
   sweet cooking
   chocolate, grated
   fine

1 teaspoon grated
   lemon rind
3 cups sifted flour
1 teaspoon baking
   powder
1 cup chopped,
   blanched almonds
¼ cup finely chopped
   candied orange or
   lemon peel

Beat eggs and sugar until light. Stir in spices, chocolate and lemon rind. Sift flour and baking powder over almonds and citron and coat fruit thoroughly. Stir into egg mixture. If dough is too soft to roll out, add a little more flour, one tablespoon at a time. Roll dough on lightly floured board to ¼-inch thickness. Cut into 3 × 1-inch sticks. Bake on greased baking sheet in moderate oven (350°F.) 10 to 12 minutes. Makes about 4½ dozen.

LECKERLI

1 cup sugar
½ cup honey
¼ teaspoon salt
2 teaspoons each
   cloves, cinnamon
¼ cup each finely
   diced candied
   orange and lemon
   peel
¼ cup finely diced
   citron

1 egg, well beaten
1 teaspoon baking
   soda
2 tablespoons brandy
1 teaspoon grated
   lemon rind
1 cup chopped
   almonds
3 cups sifted flour
¼ cup water

Bring ½ cup sugar and honey to boil over low heat; cool. Add salt, spices, fruits, and egg. Dissolve baking soda in brandy and add with lemon rind, nuts and flour. Knead until well blended. Chill 1 hour. Roll on lightly floured board to ½-inch thick rectangle. Put on cookie sheet covered with heavy waxed paper. Bake in moderate oven (325°F.) 30 minutes. While hot, brush with syrup made by cooking ½ cup sugar and ¼ cup water until mixture spins a thread (234°F. on a candy thermometer). Cut at once in 2½ × 1-inch strips. Pack in airtight container to ripen for about 5 weeks before serving. Can be frozen. Makes 72 cookies.

QUEEN CHARLOTTE'S TEA CAKES

*The recipe for these crisp wafers with subtle flavor is
from a 1778 British cookbook.*

1¾ cups all-purpose flour	2 teaspoons caraway seed, pounded
⅔ cup sugar	½ cup butter, softened
¼ teaspoon salt	1 tablespoon rose water
Grated rind of 1 lemon	1 egg

Mix first 5 ingredients. Add butter and rose water and work with pastry blender until crumbs are formed. Add egg and mix until blended. If too soft to roll, chill until firm. On floured board with floured rolling pin, roll small amounts of dough at a time to ¼-inch thickness. Cut with fancy 1½ to 2-inch cutters. With floured pancake turner, transfer to ungreased cookie sheet, leaving 1 inch between cookies. Bake in hot oven (400°F.) 7 minutes, or until cookies begin to brown around the edges. Remove from sheets to cake racks. Let stand until cold, then store airtight. Makes about 3 dozen.

CARAWAY STARS

*A Scandinavian Christmas cookie, traditionally cut in star shape. The flavor is
unusual; the cookies are delicious.*

1¾ cups flour	1 egg
1½ teaspoons baking powder	2 teaspoons caraway seed
¼ teaspoon salt	3 tablespoons brandy
½ cup butter or margarine, softened	⅓ cup confectioners' sugar
1 cup sugar	

Stir together flour, baking powder and salt; set aside. In large bowl beat together butter, sugar and egg until fluffy. Beat in caraway seed. Stir in flour mixture alternately with brandy. Chill until firm enough to roll out, 2 to 3 hours. Roll out on lightly floured surface to ⅛-inch thickness. Cut with 2¾-inch star-shaped cookie cutter. Reroll scraps. Place 1 inch apart on ungreased cookie sheets. Dust tops generously with sifted confectioners' sugar. Bake in preheated 375°F. oven 10 to 12 minutes or until lightly browned. Remove to racks to cool. Makes 60.

EIGHTEENTH-CENTURY GINGER WAFERS

2 cups all-purpose
flour (do not use
instant type)
½ teaspoon baking
soda
3 teaspoons ginger
½ teaspoon nutmeg,
freshly grated
½ cup butter or

margarine
¼ cup plus 2
tablespoons dark
molasses
½ cup packed dark-
brown sugar
2 tablespoons dairy
sour cream
Confectioners' sugar

Sift first 4 ingredients into a deep mixing bowl. In saucepan, heat butter, molasses and sugar. Stir until sugar and butter are dissolved but remove from range before mixture boils. Cool to lukewarm. Pour the warm syrup mixture into the sifted dry ingredients and stir in the sour cream. With a floured rolling pin, roll small pieces of dough on a floured board until they are as "thin as gauze," according to the eighteenth-century directions. Cut out with a floured 2-inch scalloped cookie cutter, or use any desired shape. Place on cookie sheet and bake in hot oven (400°F.) 6 to 8 minutes, or until done. Remove cookies from oven. Loosen with spatula or pancake turner. Dust with confectioners' sugar while still warm. Makes about 8 dozen small cookies. These cookies are delicious with custards, fresh or stewed fruits, or to munch between meals or at teatime.

JUMBO MOLASSES COOKIES

½ cup vegetable
shortening
Sugar
½ cup water
1 cup molasses
3½ cups unsifted all-
purpose flour
(instant type can be
used)

½ teaspoon salt
1 teaspoon soda
1½ teaspoons ginger
½ teaspoon ground
cloves
¼ teaspoon allspice
Seeded raisins

Cream shortening and 1 cup sugar until light and fluffy. Combine water and molasses. Sift flour with remaining ingredients, except raisins. Add alternately to first mixture with water and molasses, blending well after each addition. Chill overnight. Roll out a small amount of dough at a time to ⅛-inch to ¼-inch thickness. Cut with a 3-inch cookie cutter. Put on greased cookie sheets. Top each cookie with a raisin and sprinkle with sugar. Bake in moderate oven (350°F.) 10 to 12 minutes. Makes about 3 dozen.

Rolled Fruit and Filled Cookies

FILLED CUTOUT COOKIES

*A basic dough for rolled and filled cookies. Vary the filling
and use the recipe again and again.*

½ cup butter or
   margarine, softened
¾ cup sugar
2 eggs
1 teaspoon vanilla

2½ cups flour
¼ teaspoon baking
   soda
Prune Filling and/or
   red-currant jelly

With mixer cream butter, sugar, eggs and vanilla until fluffy. Stir together flour
and baking soda and blend into creamed mixture. Wrap airtight and chill
overnight. On lightly floured surface roll out dough ¹⁄₁₆-inch thick. Cut with 2¼
inch round cutter. Put half the cookies on greased cookie sheet, spread a
teaspoonful of Prune Filling and/or currant jelly on each. For a decorative effect,
use tiny heart or star cutter to cut out center from each remaining cookie. Place
over filled cookies, pressing edges together with lightly floured fingertips. Bake
in preheated 400°F. oven 8 to 10 minutes or until golden brown. Remove to rack
to cool. Makes about 48.

PRUNE FILLING Combine 2 cups cut-up moisturized pitted prunes, ½ cup
sugar and ½ cup water in saucepan. Cook and stir over medium heat until thick
and smooth, about 5 to 6 minutes. Blend in 2 teaspoons grated orange peel and 2
tablespoons orange juice.

FRAGILE HAZELNUT COOKIE SANDWICHES

The filling is apricot jam; the topping, frosting and nuts.

Cream 1 cup butter (must be butter) with ½ cup sugar until fluffy. Work in ½
pound hazelnuts (or filberts), finely ground; and 2½ cups sifted cake flour to
make a smooth dough. Chill and roll to ⅛-inch thickness between 2 sheets of
waxed paper. Cut into small rounds or diamonds. Bake on cookie sheet in
moderate oven (350°F.) 10 to 15 minutes, or until golden brown. Cool and put 2
cookies together with apricot jam. Spread with thin Lemon Frosting, and
sprinkle with chopped pistachios. Makes 40 to 50 cookie sandwiches depending
on size.

FRENCH RASPBERRY-JAM COOKIES

These cookies are rich and delicious, but a bit fragile after they are baked. It is a good idea to use a tin box to transport them in, rather than to rely on a plastic bag.

½ cup butter	¾ cup chopped
1½ cups all-purpose	almonds
flour	¼ cup heavy cream
¼ teaspoon salt	1 cup raspberry jam
½ cup sugar	or preserves

Take butter out of refrigerator and allow it to soften at room temperature. Sift flour with salt and sugar into bowl. Stir almonds into flour mixture, then add softened butter and cream. Knead thoroughly until all ingredients are well blended. Gather dough into ball, wrap in waxed paper and refrigerate until it hardens. While dough is chilling, preheat oven to 350°F. and butter 2 cookie sheets. Roll out dough either on pastry cloth or, even better, on marble slab. You will need two sizes of round cookie cutter, one about 2½ inches, the other about 1¼ inches. With larger cutter, cut out as many cookies as possible. Then, with smaller cutter, cut a circle out of the center of half the cookies. Transfer cookies to separate cookie sheets. Bake cookies with holes about 5 minutes; others, 7 to 8 minutes. Remove to racks to cool and harden. When cool, spread whole cookies with jam and top with cookie rings. Then put more jam in center to fill up hole. Reroll dough from cutout centers and make a second batch. Makes about 1 dozen. **NOTE:** This recipe can be doubled.

SWEDISH FILLED BUTTER COOKIES
(Dubbla Mördegskakor)

Prepare recipe for Mördegskakor; chill. Roll out dough quite thin on floured board. Cut in 2½-inch rounds (use a doughnut cutter with removable center if possible), cutting half the cookies with holes in the center. Brush those with center hole with slightly beaten egg white and sprinkle with 2 tablespoons coarse sugar and 20 chopped blanched almonds. Put on greased cookie sheet and bake in moderate oven (375°F.) about 10 minutes, or until lightly browned. When ready to use, spread the cookies without holes with jelly (red currant or apple or green mint for a Christmasy effect). Put cookies with holes on top. Makes about 50.

APRICOT TURNOVERS

(shown on plates 4 and 5)

Cut-out cookies filled with preserves.

½ cup butter or margarine, softened	1¼ cups flour
¼ cup sugar	About ½ cup apricot or other preserves
1 teaspoon vanilla	1 tablespoon milk
⅛ teaspoon salt	¼ cup finely chopped nuts
1 egg, separated	

In large bowl of mixer cream butter, sugar, vanilla and salt until fluffy. Add egg white and beat well. Gradually stir in flour until blended. Wrap dough airtight and chill 1 hour or longer. Divide dough in half. Reserve half in refrigerator. On lightly floured surface roll out dough about ⅛-inch thick. Cut out 3-inch round cookies; place ½-inch apart on lightly greased cookie sheet. Repeat with reserved half of dough. Spoon about ½ teaspoon preserves on center of each cookie. Fold in half and press edges to seal. Beat egg yolk and milk and brush on turnovers. Sprinkle with nuts. Bake in preheated 350°F. oven 10 to 12 minutes or until golden. Remove to rack to cool. Makes about 30.

DANISH SPICE COOKIES

A two-layered cookie filled with apricot preserves.

1 cup soft butter or margarine	1 teaspoon salt
½ cup dark-brown sugar, packed	1 teaspoon baking soda
½ cup granulated sugar	1 teaspoon each cinnamon and ginger
⅓ cup molasses	½ teaspoon cloves
⅔ cup light corn syrup	Apricot preserves
4½ cups sifted flour	Candied-cherry halves

Cream butter and sugars until light. Beat in molasses and corn syrup. Add sifted dry ingredients and mix well. Chill until firm enough to roll. Roll half of dough to ½-inch thickness and cut with 3-inch round cutter. Roll remaining half of dough to ⅛-inch thickness and cut with 3-inch daisy or other fancy cutter. Bake all cookies in moderate oven (375°F.) about 8 minutes. Cool. Spread round cookies with preserves and top with fancy cookies. Press a cherry half in center. Makes 48.

BOHEMIAN KOLACKY

A Czechoslovakian cookie made from a rich cream-cheese dough.

2 cups flour
2 tablespoons sugar
2 teaspoons baking
 powder
½ teaspoon salt
1 cup butter or
 margarine, softened

9 ounces cream
 cheese, softened
2 medium-size eggs,
 well beaten
½ cup cherry or
 apricot preserves

Stir together flour, sugar, baking powder and salt; set aside. In large bowl cream butter and cheese until well blended. Stir in flour mixture. Add eggs, mixing to form stiff dough. Chill until firm enough to roll out, several hours or overnight. Roll out a fourth of dough at a time on lightly floured surface, preferably with stockinette-covered rolling pin, to slightly less than ¼-inch thickness. (Keep remainder chilled.) Cut in rounds with floured 1¾-inch cutter. Reroll scraps. With floured index finger make deep indentation in center of each. Fill with scant measuring ¼ teaspoon preserves (if you use too much, it will bubble up and spill onto cookie while it bakes, spoiling its appearance). Place 1 inch apart on ungreased cookie sheets. Bake in preheated 375°F. oven about 15 minutes or until golden. Remove to racks to cool. Makes 78.

SWEDISH MARMALADE COOKIES
(Syltkakor)

¾ cup butter or
 margarine
Sugar
2 eggs, well beaten
1 teaspoon vanilla
3½ cups all-purpose
 flour (instant type
 can be used)

3 teaspoons baking
 powder
½ teaspoon salt
⅓ cup light cream
Marmalade or
 preserves

Cream butter until light. Add 1 cup sugar, eggs and vanilla. Mix dry ingredients and add alternately with cream. Chill. Roll out on lightly floured board to about ⅛-inch thickness. Cut with 2½-inch round cutter. Put about ½ teaspoon of marmalade on half the rounds, top with remaining cookies and press around edges with a fork. Prick tops, sprinkle with sugar and put on greased cookie sheet. Bake in moderate oven (375°F.) 10 to 12 minutes. Makes about 7 dozen.

RAISIN-FILLED COOKIES

½ cup butter or
    margarine, softened
¾ cup sugar
1 egg
½ teaspoon vanilla
1½ cups all-purpose
    flour

¼ teaspoon salt
¼ teaspoon baking
    powder
1 tablespoon cream or
    milk
Raisin Filling

Cream butter. Gradually add sugar and beat until light. Beat in egg and vanilla. Add dry ingredients and cream and mix well. Chill several hours, or until firm enough to roll. Then roll a small amount at a time to ⅛-inch thickness on lightly floured cloth or board and cut in 3-inch rounds. (Keep remaining dough refrigerated while rolling.) Put half the rounds on cookie sheet and top each with a teaspoonful of filling. Top with remaining rounds. With floured fork, press edges together and prick tops. Bake in hot oven (400°F.) 10 to 12 minutes. Makes about 1½ dozen.

RAISIN FILLING In saucepan, mix ½ cup sugar, 1 tablespoon flour and dash of salt. Add ½ cup water and 1 cup chopped seeded raisins. Cook, stirring, until thickened and blended. Add 1 teaspoon grated lemon rind and cool. Makes about 1 cup.

FILLED OATMEAL COOKIES

1 cup soft butter or
    margarine
1 cup sugar
1 teaspoon vanilla
2 cups rolled oats,
    ground very fine

2 cups sifted flour
¼ teaspoon baking
    soda
¾ teaspoon salt
½ cup buttermilk
Date-Nut Filling

Cream butter with sugar and vanilla. Add oats and sifted flour, baking soda and salt alternately with buttermilk; mix well. Chill several hours. Roll very thin; cut with small cookie cutters. Bake in hot oven (400°F.) 8 to 10 minutes. Put together in pairs with filling the day cookies are served. (Or fill, wrap and freeze.) Makes about 7 dozen small finished cookies.

DATE-NUT FILLING Cut 1 pound pitted dates in small pieces. Put in saucepan with 1½ cups sugar, ½ teaspoon salt, 2 teaspoons grated lemon rind and 2 cups water. Bring to boil and cook 10 minutes, or until thickened, stirring occasionally. Add 2 cups finely chopped nuts and cool.

ISCHELER TORTELETTES

One of the most famous of all Austrian cookies.

2 cups sifted flour
½ teaspoon baking powder
¼ teaspoon salt
Sweet butter. (Must be butter; if salted butter is used, omit salt.)
1 cup ground, blanched almonds
¾ cup sugar
1 tablespoon lemon juice
Grated rind of
1 lemon
½ cup apricot jam
4 ounces semi-sweet chocolate pieces
Blanched almonds, halved

Sift flour with baking powder and salt. Cut 1 cup butter in small pieces. Add butter, ground almonds, sugar, lemon juice and rind to flour. Knead with hands until dough is very smooth and firm. Chill for at least 2 hours. Roll small parts of dough between waxed paper to ⅛- to ¼-inch thickness; keep remaining dough chilled until using. Cut into 1- or 2-inch rounds. Bake cookies on greased and floured cookie sheets in moderate oven (350°F.) 10 minutes, or until golden. Remove cookies carefully. Very thin cookies are fragile. After cooling, put two cookies together with jam, sandwich fashion. Melt chocolate and 1 tablespoon butter over hot, not boiling, water. Beat until smooth. If necessary, add up to 1 tablespoon hot water to achieve spreading consistency. Frost tortelettes on top and sides. Place half an almond on center of each cookie while frosting is still soft. Makes about 5 dozen 1-inch tortelettes or about 2½ dozen 2-inch tortelettes.

RAISIN-NUT PINWHEELS

This cookie is twice rolled—a filling of raisins, nuts and orange marmalade is rolled up in a sheet of dough.

1 cup soft butter or margarine
½ cup sugar
1 egg
2 cups sifted flour
1 teaspoon baking powder
1 cup commercial sour cream
Raisin-Nut Filling

Cream butter and sugar until light. Beat in egg. Add sifted dry ingredients alternately with sour cream, beating until smooth. Chill overnight. Roll one-fourth of dough at a time on well-floured board or pastry cloth to form a rectangle 10 inches × 6 inches. (Dough will be soft. Keep in refrigerator until ready to use.) Spread with one-fourth of filling and roll up from 10-inch side. Cut in 12 pieces and put, cut side up, 3 inches apart, on greased sheet. Bake in moderate oven (350°F.) about 15 minutes. Repeat until all ingredients are used. Makes 4 dozen.

Filling: Mix 1 cup chopped nuts, ¼ cup raisins, ¾ cup orange marmalade, ¼ cup sugar and 1 teaspoon ground cinnamon.

VI
REFRIGERATOR
COOKIES

One of the joys of refrigerator cookies is the way they work into a busy schedule without imposing on your time. These are the "stop-and-start" champions, par excellence. And if baking a large batch of cookies seems too ambitious an endeavor, bake up a few dozen refrigerator cookies and chill the rest of the dough for another day. Freeze dough if that is more convenient; take it out in the morning, put it in the refrigerator and it will be ready to slice and bake that evening, by the time you return home from work.

Refrigerator cookies are easy to prepare. First, roll up a log of cookie dough 2 inches in diameter, or an oblong 2 inches thick, and chill it thoroughly, wrapped tightly in waxed paper or plastic. The next day (or next week), slice off however many you wish and bake them.

Thick-sliced cookies will be soft in the middle; thin-sliced ones will be crisp. And if thin is what pleases you the most, then refrigerator cookies are perfect—they slice thinner and handle more easily than if the dough were rolled out. The more thoroughly chilled the dough, the easier it will be.

For fancy edges, roll the dough in chopped nuts or colored sugar before slicing.

Even if a recipe is not specified as such, you can treat many other types of cookie doughs as if they were refrigerator cookies, provided the recipe calls for more than a quarter cup of shortening for every cup of flour. Any less than that and the dough will dry out and crumble if refrigerated.

Basic
and Delectable Doughs

FARMERS' COOKIES

1 cup butter or
   margarine, softened
¾ cup sugar
1 tablespoon
   molasses
½ cup chopped
   walnuts

1 tablespoon warm
   water
1 teaspoon baking
   soda
2½ cups all-purpose
   flour

Cream butter. Gradually add sugar and beat until light and fluffy. Stir in molasses, nuts and warm water. Mix baking soda with small amount of flour. Add to first mixture. Stir in remaining flour in 2 portions. Knead with hands just until dough holds together. Divide dough in 2 equal parts and shape each in a roll about 1½ inches in diameter. Wrap each in plastic and chill 1 hour. Cut in ¼-inch slices and put on lightly greased cookie sheets. Bake in preheated 350°F. oven 12 minutes, or until light brown and crisp. Cool on rack, then store airtight in cool place. Makes about 5½ dozen.

BUTTERSCOTCH MAPLE COOKIES

Good keepers and shippers. Brush with maple syrup before baking.

½ cup soft butter or
   margarine
½ cup light-brown
   sugar, packed
½ cup granulated
   sugar
1 egg

2½ cups sifted flour
½ teaspoon salt
½ teaspoon baking
   soda
1 teaspoon cinnamon
Maple syrup
Almond halves

Cream butter and sugars until light. Beat in egg. Sift in flour with salt, baking soda and cinnamon. Stir until mixture forms a ball. Divide dough into 3 parts. Shape each on waxed paper in a roll about 2 inches in diameter. Chill until firm. Slice in ¼-inch cookies. Put on greased sheets. Brush with maple syrup. Place almond half on each cookie. Bake in hot oven (400°F.) 10 minutes or until golden brown. Makes about 40.

BUTTERSCOTCH COOKIES

½ cup butter or margarine, softened
1 cup packed light brown sugar
1 egg
1 teaspoon vanilla

2 cups all-purpose flour
½ teaspoon baking soda
½ cup coarsely chopped walnuts

Cream butter and sugar well. Add egg and vanilla and beat until creamy. Stir in flour mixed with baking soda. Add nuts, mixing with hands if necessary. Pack in 9 × 5 × 3-inch loaf pan lined with waxed paper. Chill overnight or longer. Slice about ¼ inch thick and put on ungreased cookie sheets. Bake in 400°F. oven about 8 minutes. Makes about 3 dozen.

ANTEBELLUM BROWN-SUGAR WAFERS

These cookies should be large, round and thin. They are very crisp and almost melt in the mouth. A quantity recipe that can easily be halved.

2 cups packed light-brown sugar
1½ cups softened (not runny or whipped) butter
3 eggs
1 teaspoon vanilla

6 cups all-purpose flour (instant type can be used)
½ teaspoon each salt, baking soda and cinnamon

Cream sugar and butter, using electric mixer, if available. When blended, add eggs one at a time, beating well after each addition. Add vanilla. Mix remaining ingredients. Combine the mixtures, adding the dry ingredients gradually to the other ingredients. Do not overbeat; as soon as mixture is smooth, remove from electric mixer. Shape in 4 refrigerator rolls 2 inches in diameter. Put on cookie sheet and chill, then wrap in foil and freeze. Cut in ⅛-inch slices to bake. (If using the dough at once, chill and cut into ¼-inch slices.) With the fingers, mash dough thin and even it with palms. Or mash with the bottom of a glass tumbler. Cookies should be ⅛ inch thick or less. Place 2 inches apart on cookie sheets. Bake in hot oven (400°F.) 3 to 5 minutes, or until cookies are done inside and lightly browned; break one open to test. Remove from oven, loosen cookies with a pancake turner and let cool to room temperature before serving or storing. Store airtight. You can also roll a small amount of dough at a time and cut with scalloped cutter. Bake as above and decorate with frosting, if desired. Makes about 14 dozen. **Note:** To halve recipe use 1 whole egg and 1 yolk.

HILMA'S CHRISTMAS SLICES

Oatmeal refrigerator cookies that are rolled in multicolored candy shot. No egg in the recipe.

1 cup butter or margarine (part may be shortening)	½ teaspoon salt
½ cup confectioners' sugar	1 cup old-fashioned or quick-cooking rolled oats
2 teaspoons vanilla	Multicolored or chocolate shot
1¼ cups flour	

In large bowl of mixer cream butter and sugar until fluffy. Add vanilla. Beat in flour, salt and oats. Divide dough in half. Shape each half in log about 1 inch in diameter. Roll in colored shot. Wrap in plastic wrap or waxed paper and chill. Cut in ¼-inch slices. Bake on lightly greased cookie sheets in preheated 350°F. oven 7 to 10 minutes or until light brown. Makes about 84.

VANILLA-CURRANT COOKIES

1 cup all-purpose flour	¼ cup butter or margarine
¼ teaspoon baking powder	2 tablespoons dried currants
⅛ teaspoon salt	½ teaspoon vanilla
¼ cup sugar	1 egg

On board, mix first 4 ingredients. Cut in butter and sprinkle with currants. Add vanilla and egg and work quickly together to form a ball. Shape in a roll 12 inches long, wrap in waxed paper and chill until firm. With a sharp knife, cut roll in ¼-inch slices. Put on lightly greased cookie sheet 1 inch apart and with a fork dipped in flour make a lattice pattern on each cookie. Bake in moderate oven (375°F.) 12 to 15 minutes. Remove at once from sheet. Makes about 3 dozen.

VARIATION Omit currants and roll sliced cookies in a mixture of 1 teaspoon each sugar and cinnamon. Proceed as directed.

REFRIGERATOR COOKIES

The most basic of all doughs. For variety, roll in sugar, or cinnamon sugar, or nuts before slicing cookies.

1 cup butter, softened
2 cups packed brown
 sugar
2 eggs

3½ cups all-purpose
 flour
½ teaspoon each salt
 and baking soda

Cream butter, add sugar and beat in eggs and then remaining ingredients. Shape in rolls about 2 inches in diameter. Refrigerate overnight. Slice thin and bake in moderate oven (375°F.) 8 to 10 minutes. Makes about 12 dozen. **NOTE:** This recipe can be halved.

Chocolate Refrigerator Cookies and Variations

SWISS SEMISWEETS

A rich, delicious combination of chocolate and orange.

1 cup butter, softened
½ cup granulated
  sugar or packed
  brown sugar
2 eggs
3 tablespoons freshly
  grated orange rind
2 tablespoons orange
  juice
2¾ cups all-purpose flour

¼ teaspoon each salt
  and baking soda
⅔ cup chopped
  walnuts
1 package (8 ounces)
  semisweet
  chocolate squares,
  finely chopped or
  coarsely grated

In a large mixing bowl, cream butter and sugar together thoroughly; add eggs and beat well. Beat in orange rind and juice. Sift flour with salt and baking soda; beat into creamed mixture. Stir in nuts and chocolate. Shape dough on waxed paper into long rectangles about 1 inch square; roll up to wrap. Chill in refrigerator or freezer until firm. Slice dough in ⅛-inch thick squares. Place on greased cookie sheet and bake in moderate oven (350°F.) 9 minutes, or until golden. Remove to wire rack to cool. Makes about 8 dozen.

MARBLED COOKIES
(shown on plate 5)

Chocolate and vanilla combined in a not-too-sweet sliced cookie.

½ cup butter or
  margarine, softened
¼ cup sugar
1 teaspoon vanilla

⅛ teaspoon salt
1¼ cups flour
2 tablespoons cocoa

In large bowl of mixer cream butter, sugar, vanilla and salt until fluffy. Gradually stir in flour until blended. Divide dough in half. With hand work cocoa into one half until well blended, then with both hands roll each half in 18-inch-long rope. Twist ropes loosely together; then fold in half and shape in 9-inch roll. Wrap airtight and chill several hours or overnight. Cut in ¼-inch-thick slices. Place 1 inch apart on lightly greased cookie sheet. Bake in preheated 350°F. oven 12 to 14 minutes or until white part is golden. Remove to rack to cool. Makes about 36.

CHOCOLATE REFRIGERATOR COOKIES

Be sure to prepare dough ahead and chill overnight.

1 cup butter or margarine, softened	2 cups flour
¾ cup sugar	½ cup cocoa
1 teaspoon vanilla	1 cup chopped walnuts
¼ teaspoon salt	1 bar (4 ounces) sweet cooking chocolate, melted
1 egg	

Cream butter, sugar, vanilla and salt until light. Beat in egg. Stir in flour and cocoa until well blended. Chill dough in bowl about 2 hours or until firm enough to handle. Form 2 rolls 1½ inches in diameter. Roll in walnuts until well coated. Wrap airtight and chill overnight. Cut in ³⁄₁₆-inch slices and place 1 inch apart on lightly greased cookie sheet. Bake in 400°F. oven until crisp, 8 to 10 minutes. Remove to rack to cool. Spoon about ½ measuring teaspoon chocolate on center of each cookie, then spread to within ¼ inch of edge. Let chocolate harden. Store airtight in cool, dry place. Makes about 72.

VANILLA-CHOCOLATE CLOVERS

A tasty cookie with great visual appeal.

1 cup butter or margarine, softened	spooned into cup
¾ cup sugar	2 tablespoons cornstarch
¼ teaspoon salt	2 tablespoons cocoa
2 teaspoons vanilla	Slightly beaten egg white
2½ cups all-purpose flour, lightly	

Cream butter. Add sugar, salt and vanilla and continue creaming until light and fluffy. Mix flour with cornstarch; gradually add to first mixture. Put dough on lightly floured surface and quickly gather into ball. Divide in 2 equal portions. Add cocoa to one portion and work until cocoa is evenly mixed. Divide each portion in 4 pieces and shape in ¾-inch rolls. Brush each roll with egg white. Put 1 white roll next to 1 cocoa roll, then put 1 cocoa roll on top of white and 1 white roll on top of cocoa. Repeat with 4 remaining rolls, making 2 rolls, each consisting of 4 smaller rolls. Wrap each in waxed paper and chill well. With sharp thin-bladed knife, cut in ¼-inch slices. (Pinch rolls together if they separate while cutting.) Put on lightly greased cookie sheet and bake in moderate oven (350°F.) 8 to 10 minutes, or until white part is golden brown. Remove to rack. Makes about 60.

CHOCOLATE PINWHEEL COOKIES

1 square (1 ounce) unsweetened chocolate	¼ teaspoon baking powder	margarine, softened
1¼ cups regular all-purpose flour	¼ teaspoon salt	¾ cup sugar
	½ cup butter or	1 teaspoon vanilla
		1 egg

Over hot water or very low heat, melt chocolate; cool. Mix next 3 ingredients and set aside. Put next 4 ingredients in large bowl of electric mixer and beat until light and fluffy. Add flour mixture and stir until blended. Halve dough and add chocolate to one half. Wrap both halves in plastic and chill several hours, or until firm enough to roll. Dampen counter with water and spread with sheet of plastic wrap. Roll plain dough on lightly floured wrap to form 16 × 6-inch rectangle. Repeat with chocolate dough. Invert chocolate dough on plain dough and peel off wrap. Press gently with rolling pin. Roll up like jelly roll, being sure center is tight. Roll back and forth on counter, if necessary, to make center the same diameter as ends (about 1½ inches).Wrap in plastic and chill overnight. Preheat oven to moderate (350°F.). Slice ⅛-inch thick and bake on lightly greased cookie sheets 10 to 12 minutes, or until lightly browned. Remove at once to wire racks to cool. Makes 7½ to 8 dozen.
To Store Store airtight. Can be frozen. Good keepers but poor shippers.

FOUR-LEAF-CLOVER COOKIES

Refrigerator cookies flavored with chocolate and peanut butter.

¾ cup butter or margarine, softened	2¼ cups all-purpose flour	chocolate, melted and cooled
½ cup smooth peanut butter	1¼ teaspoons baking powder	¼ cup finely chopped peanuts
1¼ cups sugar	1 square (1 ounce) unsweetened	1 egg white, slightly beaten
1 egg		
1 teaspoon vanilla		

Cream butter and peanut butter until light and fluffy. Gradually add sugar, beating well. Beat in egg and vanilla. Combine next 2 ingredients and gradually add to first mixture. Turn out dough on lightly floured board and gather into ball. Divide dough in 2 equal parts. Work chocolate into 1 part until evenly mixed; work chopped peanuts into other. Divide each portion in 8 pieces, then shape in rolls ¾ inch in diameter, alternating chocolate and white rolls, brushing each with egg white and placing one on top of other to form logs of 4 rolls each. Roll logs in waxed paper and chill several hours, then cut in ¼-inch slices with thin, sharp-bladed knife (pinch rolls together if they separate while slicing). Put on lightly greased baking sheets and bake in preheated 350°F. oven about 10 minutes. Cool on racks. Makes about 12 dozen.

CHOCOLATE MINT COOKIES

Two popular flavors are combined in a filled cookie.

½ cup margarine	2 cups sifted flour
½ cup sugar	1 teaspoon baking
1 egg	powder
½ teaspoon vanilla	½ teaspoon salt
2 squares (2 ounces)	Mint Filling
unsweetened	Confectioners' sugar
chocolate, melted	frosting
1 tablespoon milk	Colored sugar

Cream margarine and sugar. Beat in egg, vanilla and chocolate. Add milk. Sift in flour with baking powder and salt. Shape dough in 2 rolls, 2 inches in diameter. Wrap in waxed paper and chill overnight. Cut in thin slices and bake on ungreased cookie sheet in moderate oven (350°F.) 10 minutes or until done. Cool. Spread Mint Filling on half of the cookies. Top with remaining cookies. Frost with green-tinted confectioners' sugar frosting to which a few drops of peppermint extract have been added. Sprinkle a small round of colored sugar on each. Makes about 60 double cookies.

MINT FILLING: Cream ¼ cup butter. Add 2 cups sifted confectioners' sugar a little at a time. Add a dash of salt, 1 tablespoon hot milk, ¼ teaspoon peppermint extract. Mix well.

SPICY CHOCOLATE REFRIGERATOR COOKIES

A thorough chilling, preferably overnight, guarantees perfect results.

½ cup butter or	¼ cup unsweetened
margarine, softened	cocoa
¾ cup sugar	½ teaspoon each
1 egg	baking powder and
¾ cup nuts, ground	cinnamon
in blender	¼ teaspoon ground
1¾ cups all-purpose	cloves
flour	Multicolored candies

Cream butter and sugar until light. Beat in egg, then add nuts. Mix remaining ingredients, except candies, and stir into first mixture. Divide in 2 equal parts and shape each in a roll about 1 inch in diameter. Sprinkle candies on waxed paper and coat each roll. Wrap rolls in waxed paper and chill overnight. Cut in ¼-inch slices and bake on lightly greased cookie sheets in preheated 350°F. oven about 10 minutes. Makes about 5 dozen.

Spice Cookies

CINNAMON REFRIGERATOR COOKIES

A favorite spice in an easily prepared cookie.

2¼ cups flour
½ cup granulated
  sugar
1 cup butter or
  margarine

1 egg, separated
3 tablespoons packed
  brown sugar mixed
  with 1 teaspoon
  cinnamon

In mixing bowl combine flour and granulated sugar. With fork cut in butter until particles are size of peas. Add egg yolk and mix dough with hands until smooth. Divide in half and shape in 2 logs about 1½ inches in diameter. Brush with slightly beaten egg white and roll in brown-sugar mixture. Chill 1 hour, then cut in ¼-inch slices. Bake on greased cookie sheet in preheated 350°F. oven 12 to 15 minutes or until golden. Remove to rack to cool. Makes about 60.

GINGERSNAPS

*Less time consuming than the rolled variety. An easy
recipe for quantity baking.*

½ cup dark corn
  syrup
1 cup granulated
  sugar
2 teaspoons
  cinnamon
2 teaspoons ground
  cloves

3 teaspoons ginger
1 cup butter or
  margarine, softened
1½ teaspoons baking
  soda
4½ cups all-purpose
  flour

Combine ½ cup water and first 5 ingredients in small saucepan and bring to boil. Pour over butter and stir until cool. Mix baking soda and 4 cups flour. Gradually add to first mixture and stir until well blended. Cover and chill overnight. Divide dough in 6 to 8 parts and roll each part thin on lightly floured board, using remaining flour. Cut out with scalloped or round cookie cutter and put on ungreased cookie sheet. Reroll leftover dough. Bake in preheated 375°F. oven 6 to 7 minutes, or until well browned. Let cool on sheets. Store in airtight containers in a dry place. Makes about 16 dozen 2½-inch cookies.

LINZER SPICE COOKIES

A marvelous holiday cookie, delicious at any time of year.

⅔ cup filberts
1½ cups flour
2 teaspoons cinnamon
1 teaspoon baking powder
½ teaspoon cloves
¼ teaspoon salt
1 cup butter or margarine, softened
1 cup sugar
4 teaspoons grated orange peel (about 2 large oranges)
2 teaspoons grated lemon peel (1 large lemon)
2 egg yolks

Spread filberts in shallow pan; toast in preheated 350°F. oven 6 minutes, stirring or shaking occasionally. Rub filberts in towel or between fingers to remove skins; cool. Grind in blender or food processor until fine; set aside. Mix flour, cinnamon, baking powder, cloves and salt; set aside. In large bowl of mixer cream butter and sugar until light. Beat in orange and lemon peels and egg yolks until fluffy. Gradually stir in flour mixture. Stir in filberts. Chill until firm enough to handle, about 2 hours. On lightly floured surface shape dough in 2 logs about 1½ inches thick. Wrap in waxed paper; chill until firm, several hours or overnight. Slice ³⁄₁₆ inch thick. Bake ½ inch apart on ungreased cookie sheet in preheated 350°F. oven until golden, 9 to 12 minutes (watch carefully so as not to burn). Remove at once to racks; cool. Makes 86 to 108.

CARDAMOM-CINNAMON SQUARES

Spicy sliced cookies.

1¼ cups flour
1 teaspoon cinnamon
½ teaspoon crushed cardamon seed or ground cardamom
⅛ teaspoon salt
½ cup butter or margarine, softened
¼ cup packed brown sugar

Stir together flour, cinnamon, cardamom and salt; set aside. In large bowl of mixer cream butter and sugar until fluffy. Gradually stir in flour mixture until blended. With hands shape dough in 8-inch-long log with 1½-inch-square sides. Wrap airtight and chill several hours or overnight. Slice ³⁄₁₆ inch thick and place squares 1 inch apart on ungreased cookie sheet. Bake in preheated 350°F. oven 12 to 14 minutes or until light brown. Remove to rack to cool. Makes about 36.

NUTMEG ROUNDS

(shown on plate 4)

Tender sliced cookies made in a jiffy.

½ cup butter or
   margarine, softened
6 tablespoons sugar,
   divided
1 teaspoon vanilla
⅛ teaspoon salt
1¼ cups flour

1 egg or egg white,
   slightly beaten
1 teaspoon nutmeg
Slivered almonds,
   raisins or chopped
   candied fruits
   (optional)

In large bowl of mixer cream butter, 4 tablespoons sugar, vanilla and salt until fluffy. Stir in flour until blended. With hands shape dough in 9-inch roll. Brush with egg and roll in mixture of remaining 2 tablespoons sugar and the nutmeg. Wrap airtight and chill several hours or overnight. Cut in ¼-inch slices and place 1 inch apart on lightly greased cookie sheet. Press almond sliver on center of each. Bake in preheated 350°F. oven 12 to 14 minutes or until golden. Remove to rack to cool. Makes about 30.

ALMOND-SPICE SLICES

So delicious they will surely fill the cookie jar again and again.

1 cup butter or
   margarine, softened
1 cup light-brown
   sugar, lightly
   packed
2 tablespoons
   molasses
1 egg
2 teaspoons
   cinnamon
1 teaspoon ginger

1 teaspoon ground
   cardamom
1 cup coarsely
   chopped blanched
   almonds
4 cups sifted all-
   purpose flour
¼ teaspoon salt
1 teaspoon baking
   soda
Green sugar

Cream butter. Add brown sugar and molasses, creaming until fluffy. Add eggs, spices and almonds and mix well. Sift next 3 ingredients and stir about one fourth at a time into first mixture. Turn out on lightly floured board and work until smooth. Divide in 2 pieces and shape each piece in roll 6 inches long. Flatten each piece to a rectangle 6 inches long, 3 inches wide and 1½ inches thick and coat surface with green sugar. Wrap in waxed paper and chill well. With sharp knife, cut in ⅛-inch slices. Bake on lightly greased cookie sheet in slow oven (325°F.) 12 to 14 minutes. Makes about 6 dozen.

Nut Cookies

CRISP NUT SLICES

Good snack cookies that keep and ship well.

½ cup butter or
  margarine, softened
½ cup sugar
1 tablespoon
  molasses
⅛ teaspoon salt

⅓ cup finely chopped
  nuts
1½ cups flour
½ teaspoon baking
  soda

Cream butter, sugar, molasses and salt until fluffy. Stir in nuts. Stir together flour and baking soda. Gradually stir into creamed mixture until blended. With hands shape dough in 10-inch roll. Wrap airtight and chill 1 hour or longer. With sharp knife cut in ³⁄₁₆-inch-thick slices. Place 1 inch apart on lightly greased cookie sheet. Bake in preheated 350°F. oven 8 to 10 minutes or until light brown and crisp. Remove to rack to cool. Makes about 50.

REFRIGERATOR NUT COOKIES

Dough will keep in refrigerator up to 1 month. Slice and bake as needed.

1 cup margarine,
  softened
1 cup packed light-
  brown sugar
2 eggs
2 teaspoons vanilla

2¾ cups flour mixed
  with ½ teaspoon
  each salt and
  baking soda
1 cup finely chopped
  walnuts, divided

In large bowl of mixer beat margarine, sugar, eggs and vanilla until light and fluffy. Stir in flour mixture until well mixed. Stir in ½ cup walnuts. Cover and chill at least 1 hour. Turn dough onto lightly floured sheet of waxed paper. With lightly floured hands mold into roll 15 inches long. Roll in remaining ½ cup walnuts. Wrap securely in waxed paper, plastic wrap or foil and chill several hours or overnight. With sharp knife, cut desired number of ⅛-inch-thick slices. Bake on ungreased cookie sheet in preheated 400°F. oven 6 to 8 minutes or until lightly browned around edges. Good served warm. Makes about 120.

CRISP ALMOND GINGERSNAPS

1 cup butter or
  margarine, softened
1 cup sugar
½ cup dark corn
  syrup
2 teaspoons each
  cinnamon, cloves
  and ginger

1 teaspoon baking
  soda
1 cup chopped
  blanched almonds
3 cups flour

Combine butter, sugar, syrup, spices and baking soda in large bowl of electric mixer. Beat until well blended and light. Stir in almonds and flour. On lightly floured surface shape dough in 2 logs about 10 inches long. Wrap airtight and chill overnight. Cut in ⅜-inch slices and bake on greased cookie sheets in preheated 325°F. oven until light brown, about 10 minutes. Remove to rack to cool. Store in airtight container in cool, dry place. Makes 72.

SLICED WALNUT SHORTBREADS

Rich, tender butter cookies.

2¼ cups all-purpose
  flour
¼ teaspoon salt
½ cup confectioners'
  sugar
1 cup butter or
  margarine

2 teaspoons vanilla
1¼ cups finely
  chopped walnuts,
  divided
1 egg white, slightly
  beaten

Combine and mix well first 3 ingredients. Cut in butter until particles are the size of peas. Sprinkle with vanilla and ¾ cup walnuts and quickly assemble particles with hands to form ball. Divide dough in 2 equal pieces and shape each in roll 1½ inches in diameter. Brush with egg white, then roll in remaining nuts (colored green, if desired; see below), pressing nuts into rolls. Cover with waxed paper and chill. Cut in ¼-inch slices and put on ungreased cookie sheets. Bake in preheated 400°F. oven 10 minutes, or until light golden brown. Cool on racks. Makes about 5 dozen.
TO MAKE GREEN WALNUTS. Put ½ cup finely chopped walnuts in small plastic bag with 2 drops green food coloring and ¼ teaspoon water. Close bag and work with hands until an even light green color is obtained.

SWEDISH ALMOND COOKIES
(Mandelkakor)

2 cups all-purpose
  flour (instant type
  can be used)
½ cup potato flour or
  cornstarch
1 teaspoon salt
1 cup butter

1 cup sugar
1 teaspoon almond
  extract
1 cup chopped
  blanched almonds
1 egg white, slightly
  beaten

Sift flour, potato flour and salt onto board. Add butter, sugar, extract and ½ cup almonds. Form into rolls about 1½ inches in diameter. Chill. Brush rolls with egg white and roll in remaining almonds. Cut in ¼-inch slices and put on greased cookie sheet. Bake in moderate oven (375°F.) 12 to 15 minutes. Makes about 6 dozen.

Fruit and Nut Cookies

LEMON-NUT SLICES

Dough will keep in refrigerator up to 2 weeks. Slice off and bake as many cookies as desired for fresh-baked eating.

1¼ cups flour	1 egg
¼ teaspoon baking powder	1 tablespoon grated lemon peel
⅛ teaspoon salt	½ cup finely chopped nuts (almonds, pecans, walnuts)
½ cup margarine	
½ cup sugar	

Mix well flour, baking powder and salt; set aside. In large bowl of mixer cream margarine. Gradually beat in sugar, then egg and lemon peel. Stir in flour mixture and nuts. On lightly floured surface shape dough in 12-inch roll. Wrap tight and chill at least 5 hours. Slice ¼ inch thick; place on ungreased cookie sheet. Bake in preheated 400°F. oven 8 to 10 minutes or until edges are light brown. Makes about 48.

APRICOT-PECAN SLICES

1 cup butter or margarine, softened	½ cup minced dried apricots
½ cup granulated sugar	½ cup finely chopped pecans
½ cup light corn syrup	3½ cups sifted all-purpose flour
¼ teaspoon salt	Red and yellow sugar
1 teaspoon almond extract	

Cream butter. Add granulated sugar and corn syrup and continue creaming until light and fluffy. Stir in next 4 ingredients. Stir in flour about one fourth at a time and shape mixture in ball. Divide in 4 equal parts and shape each in 1½-inch roll. Coat in mixture of equal parts of red and yellow sugar. Wrap in waxed paper and chill well. Cut in ¼-inch slices with sharp thin-bladed knife. Put on cookie sheet and bake in moderate oven (350°F.) 12 to 15 minutes. Remove to rack. Makes about 8 dozen.

MEXICAN CHRISTMAS COOKIES
(Biscochos)

Delicious orange and nut cookies.

1 cup vegetable shortening
1¼ cups granulated sugar
Slightly beaten egg
2 teaspoons grated orange rind
⅓ cup fresh orange juice

½ cup finely chopped pecans
4 cups sifted all-purpose flour
¼ teaspoon salt
1 teaspoon cinnamon
½ teaspoon ground cloves
Very fine sugar

Cream shortening and granulated sugar until light. Blend in next 4 ingredients. Sift flour with salt and spices. Stir into first mixture and work until smooth. Chill overnight. Next day, roll out small amounts at a time on lightly floured surface to ⅛-inch thickness. Cut in desired shapes with fancy cookie cutter. Bake on lightly greased cookie sheet in moderate oven (375°F.) 8 to 10 minutes, or until golden brown. Roll in very fine sugar while still warm. Makes about 10 dozen.

Extra-Nutritious Combination Cookies

REFRIGERATOR OATMEAL COOKIES

The popular combination of oatmeal, raisins and nuts in one of the easiest versions to make.

¾ cup granulated
sugar
3½ cups light-brown
sugar, packed
1½ cups margarine,
melted
4 eggs, beaten
2 cups quick-cooking
oats

4 cups sifted flour
2 teaspoons baking
soda
2 teaspoons
cinnamon
½ teaspoon salt
1 cup chopped nuts
2 cups seedless
raisins

Mix sugars and margarine. Add eggs and oats. Stir in flour sifted with baking soda, cinnamon and salt. Add nuts and raisins and mix well. Pack into 2 waxed-paper-lined 9 × 5 × 3-inch loaf plans. Chill thoroughly. When ready to bake, turn out of pans and remove paper. Slice ¼ inch thick; put on ungreased sheets. Bake in 350°F. oven 10 minutes. Makes 5 dozen cookies.

SPICY HIGH-FIBER REFRIGERATOR COOKIES

½ cup butter,
softened
½ cup honey
1 egg
1½ cups whole-wheat
flour

1 tablespoon
cinnamon
1 teaspoon ginger
¼ teaspoon nutmeg
⅛ teaspoon cloves
½ teaspoon salt
1½ teaspoons vanilla

Cream butter and honey until fluffy, about 10 minutes. Add egg and blend well. Stir together flour, spices and salt. Add to creamed mixture with vanilla, blending well. On 12 × 12-inch piece of waxed paper shape dough in 10-inch log, using paper to roll even. Refrigerate 4 hours or longer. Slice very thin (³⁄₁₆ inch). Bake on ungreased cookie sheet in preheated 350°F. oven 6 to 8 minutes or until slightly brown around edges. Makes 5 dozen.

BRAN REFRIGERATOR COOKIES

Crisp butterscotch cookies.

1 cup butter or margarine, softened	1 cup chopped walnuts or pecans
2 cups packed light-brown sugar	3 cups all-purpose flour
1 egg	2 teaspoons baking powder
1 cup whole-bran cereal	

Cream butter, then gradually add sugar and beat until light and fluffy. Add eggs and beat well. Stir in bran and nuts. Mix flour with baking powder and add gradually to mixture (use hands toward end if necessary). Line two 9 × 5 × 3-inch loaf pans with waxed paper over tops to cover. Chill overnight, or a few days, if preferred. Remove from pans and cut in slices about ¼ inch thick. Using spatula, transfer to ungreased cookie sheets about 1 inch apart. Bake in preheated 400°F. oven 8 minutes, or until lightly browned. Cool on racks. Makes about 6½ dozen.

REFRIGERATOR DATE COOKIES

Prepare dough early in the day to allow thorough chilling.

1¾ cups flour	½ teaspoon vanilla
½ teaspoon baking soda	¾ cup cut-up dates
¼ teaspoon salt	½ cup finely chopped pecans
½ cup butter or margarine, softened	Whole strawberries, sprinkled with confectioners' sugar if desired
1 cup packed light-brown sugar	Fresh Lemon Ice Cream
1 egg	

Stir together flour, baking soda and salt; set aside. In large bowl of mixer cream butter and sugar until fluffy. Stir in flour mixture. Stir in dates and pecans. Shape in 2 firm logs, each 1½ inches in diameter. Wrap airtight; chill until firm, about 8 hours. Slice about ⅛ inch thick. Place on lightly greased cookie sheet. Bake in preheated 375°F. oven until rich golden brown, 8 to 10 minutes. Remove to racks to cool. Makes about 84.

PEANUT-BUTTER AND HONEY COOKIES

2½ cups flour
1½ teaspoons baking powder
½ teaspoon salt
¼ teaspoon baking soda
½ cup shortening

½ cup peanut butter
½ cup packed brown sugar
½ cup honey
1 egg
½ teaspoon vanilla
¾ cup raisins

Stir together flour, baking powder, salt and baking soda; set aside. Cream shortening and peanut butter until light and fluffy. Beat in sugar, honey, egg and vanilla until well mixed. Stir in flour mixture and raisins. Shape in roll 12 inches long; wrap and chill thoroughly. Cut in ¼-inch slices. Bake on ungreased cookie sheet in preheated 400°F. oven 8 to 10 minutes or just until edges are slightly brown. Makes about 60.

SESAME REFRIGERATOR COOKIES

½ cup butter or margarine
¾ cup sugar
1 egg
Toasted sesame seeds (about ½ cup) (see below)

2 cups all-purpose flour
1 teaspoon baking powder
¼ teaspoon salt

Cream butter until light; gradually add sugar while creaming. Add egg and beat until well mixed. Stir in ⅓ cup sesame seeds. Mix flour with the baking powder and salt. Add to mixture alternately with 2 tablespoons cold water. Mix well. Press evenly into 9 × 5 × 3-inch loaf pan lined with waxed paper. Cover and refrigerate overnight or longer. Turn out on board and peel off paper. Slice in half lengthwise, then cut in slices about ⅛-inch thick. Put on greased cookie sheets and sprinkle with remaining seeds, pressing down into dough. Bake in preheated 350°F. oven 12 minutes, or until lightly browned. Makes about 7 dozen.

TO TOAST SEEDS: Spread seeds on cookie sheet and bake at 350°F. for 10 to 15 minutes or spread seeds in a dry, heavy frying pan over moderate heat for 3 to 5 minutes, stirring occasionally. Remove immediately from pan when light brown.

DATE-NUT PINWHEELS

An old-time icebox cookie favored during the holidays, though made the year round.

4 cups flour	3 eggs
1 teaspoon salt	2 cups chopped pitted
½ teaspoon baking	dates (1 pound)
soda	1 cup granulated
1 cup shortening	sugar
2 cups packed brown	1 cup water
sugar	1 cup chopped pecans

Stir together flour, salt and baking soda; set aside. In large bowl cream shortening and brown sugar until light and fluffy. Add eggs one at a time, beating well after each. Add flour mixture; mix well; cover; chill overnight. In heavy saucepan cook dates, granulated sugar and water over low heat, stirring frequently, 10 minutes or until thickened. Remove from heat; cool; stir in pecans; set aside. Divide dough in half. On well-floured surface roll one half to 16 × 12-inch rectangle. Spread to edges with half the date-nut mixture. Roll up from long side like jelly roll. Wrap in waxed paper; chill overnight. Before baking, using a thin sharp knife, cut rolls into slices slightly less than ¼ inch thick. Place about 1 inch apart on greased cookie sheets. Bake in preheated 400°F. oven 8 to 10 minutes or until lightly browned. Remove to racks to cool. Makes 120.

VII
HAND-SHAPED
COOKIES

Ask an expert baker what type of cookie he or she enjoys the most and chances are it will be something shaped by hand. If cookie-baking is a pleasure, then hand-shaped cookies are even more so.

Whether the dough is worked at room temperature or chilled, rolled out or sliced, the final shaping is always done by hand.

Bake these cookies when you are rested and there is peace and quiet in the house. Just like any creative endeavor, the right frame of mind counts for everything, and, as the process of molding crescents, balls, logs and other shapes begins, you must be ready to enjoy it—unrushed and uninterrupted.

To assure a delicate flavor and tender, light texture, handle the dough gingerly, just enough to form the cookies and no more.

Sugar-and-Butter Cookies

TENDER SUGAR FINGERS

Easy hand-shaped cookies, good with fruit or ice cream.

½ cup butter or margarine, softened	1 teaspoon vanilla
Confectioners' sugar	⅛ teaspoon salt
	1 cup flour

Cream butter, ¼ cup sugar, vanilla and salt until fluffy. Gradually stir in flour until blended. Wrap dough airtight and chill 20 minutes or until firm enough to handle. Pinch off walnut-size pieces and roll in 3-inch fingers, using small amount of sugar on hands only if dough is sticky. Place 2 inches apart on ungreased cookie sheet. Bake in preheated 375°F. oven 10 to 12 minutes or until golden. While still slightly warm, roll in sugar. Cool completely on rack. Makes about 24.

LITTLE BUTTER S's

½ cup butter, softened	1 egg white, slightly beaten with 1 tablespoon water
⅓ cup sugar	2 tablespoons finely minced unblanched almonds mixed with 1 tablespoon sugar
3 egg yolks, well beaten	
2 tablespoons milk	
¼ teaspoon salt	
1¾ cups regular all-purpose flour	

Cream butter. Add sugar and egg yolks and beat until light. Stir in milk, salt and flour until well blended. With lightly floured hands, gather dough into ball and chill well. Preheat oven to slow (325°F.) Divide dough in 8 equal pieces and roll on lightly floured board into thin ropes less than ½ inch thick. Cut in 3½-inch pieces, taper off ends and form in S shapes. While still on board, brush with egg-white mixture and press lightly into almond-sugar mixture. Put on lightly greased cookie sheets and bake 15 to 20 minutes. Remove to rack to cool. Makes about 3 dozen.

TO STORE Store airtight in cool place. Can be frozen. Good keepers but poor shippers.

JEWEL-BROOCH COOKIES

*These cookies, French in origin, are among the most delicious of
all butter cookies. They make a perfect accompaniment for eggnog or
punch as well as an elegant dessert. French amandines, an excellent variation,
follows the recipe below.*

1 cup plus 2 tablespoons all-purpose flour (instant type can be used)	½ cup softened (not runny or whipped) butter
⅓ cup sugar	1 egg yolk
	½ teaspoon vanilla
	Garnishes

Mix flour and sugar. Add butter and mix as a piecrust until coarse crumbs are formed. Add egg yolk and vanilla and mix with the fingers or a pastry blender until dough holds together. Form into a ball and place in the refrigerator 20 minutes, or until stiff enough to handle. Using a measuring half-teaspoon, put pieces of dough 1 inch apart on cookie sheet, then shape in balls with floured palms. Make an indentation in the center of each ball with the little finger but do not punch all the way to the pan. Press one of the garnishes suggested below into the small hole. Bake in moderate oven (350°F.) 15 to 20 minutes, or until cookies are golden brown. Remove from oven and loosen cookies with a spatula. Let remain in pans until at room temperature. Store airtight at room temperature or freeze.

GARNISHES Crystallized cherries cut in quarters, stiff jam or jelly (seeded black- or red-raspberry jam is delicious), bits of candied ginger, tiny cubes of candied orange or lemon peel or citron, semisweet chocolate pieces, almond halves. You can also bake cookies without filling centers, then put a dab of chocolate frosting into the depression of cooled cookies and press a blanched-almond half into the frosting. These are called Black-Eyed Susans.

FRENCH AMANDINES Substitute ¼ cup ground almonds for ¼ cup flour in the basic recipe. Flavor with ¼ teaspoon each almond and vanilla extract. Form half-teaspoonfuls of dough into tiny sausage shapes. Bake and roll in confectioner's sugar. Makes about 4 dozen.

VANILLA PRETZELS

Crisp cookies—time-consuming but worth the effort.

2⅓ cups all-purpose
flour
¾ cup sugar
¼ teaspoon salt
1 teaspoon baking
powder

¾ cup butter or
margarine
1 egg, slightly beaten
2 teaspoons vanilla
1 egg yolk
½ cup finely chopped
nuts

Combine first 4 ingredients in mixing bowl. Cut in butter until particles are fine. Combine and beat next 2 ingredients and 2 tablespoons ice water. Sprinkle over first mixture and stir to mix. Quickly gather particles together in ball with hands. Wrap in waxed paper and chill 1 hour or longer. Divide dough in 4 equal pieces. Working with 1 piece at a time and leaving remainder in refrigerator, shape dough in roll 1 inch in diameter; cut off ¾-inch pieces. On lightly floured board, roll out pieces to pencil thickness about 8 inches long. Shape in pretzels. Brush with egg yolk beaten with 1 tablespoon water and dip in nuts. Put on lightly greased cookie sheets and bake in preheated 350°F. oven 15 minutes, or until light golden. Remove to racks to cool. Makes about 4 dozen.

GOLD COOKIES

A basic sugar cookie, rolled in nuts and cinnamon before baking.

½ cup soft butter or
margarine
1 cup sugar
4 egg yolks
1 teaspoon vanilla
1½ cups sifted flour

2 teaspoons baking
powder
1 cup finely chopped
nuts
4 teaspoons
cinnamon

Cream butter and sugar until light. Beat in egg yolks and vanilla. Stir in sifted dry ingredients. Mix nuts and cinnamon. Shape dough in ¾-inch balls and roll in nut mixture. Put on cookie sheets and bake in moderate oven (375°F.) 12 to 15 minutes. Makes about 5 dozen.

RUM BUTTER COOKIES

Rich in butter and egg yolks, these cookies with their delicate rum flavor are a holiday delight.

1 cup soft butter or margarine	2½ tablespoons rum
Sugar	2½ cups unsifted flour
3 egg yolks	1½ tablespoons powdered dried orange peel
½ teaspoon vanilla	
¼ teaspoon almond extract	

Cream butter and ¾ cup sugar until light. Beat in egg yolks, flavorings and rum. Gradually add flour, kneading in last cup. When smooth, shape in rolls about the size of a silver dollar, wrap in waxed paper and store in refrigerator overnight. Cut in ¼-inch slices and roll each slice between hands to form a ball. Mix ¼ cup sugar and the orange peel. Roll balls in this mixture, put on cookie sheet and flatten with a tumbler dipped in the sugar-orange mixture. Bake in moderate oven (350°F.) 10 to 12 minutes. Store airtight a day or two to bring out the rum flavor. Makes about 5 dozen cookies.

NOTE: For a less sugary cookie, omit rolling cookie balls in the sugar mixture. Simply flatten balls with tumbler dipped in sugar-orange mixture.

MEXICAN WEDDING COOKIES

1 cup butter or margarine, softened	1 teaspoon vanilla
Confectioners' sugar	¼ teaspoon salt
	2 cups flour

Cream butter, ½ cup sugar, vanilla and salt until fluffy. Stir in flour until well blended. Chill 30 minutes or until firm enough to handle. Shape in 1-inch balls. Place 1 inch apart on ungreased cookie sheet and bake in preheated 375°F. oven until light golden, 12 to 15 minutes. Remove to rack (close to each other) and while cookies are still warm, sift heavily with confectioners' sugar. Cool, then store airtight in cool, dry place. Before serving sift cookies with more confectioners' sugar. Makes about 48. **NOTE:** If desired, stir in 1 cup very finely chopped pecans with flour. However, these cookies will not be so tender as plain cookies.

CHRISTMAS WREATHS

These delicious Christmas cookies come from Germany. Include a few in your gift box of mixed holiday confections.

1 cup softened (not runny or whipped) butter
1 cup confectioners' sugar
Grated rind of 1 lemon
¼ cup dark Jamaica rum
3 hard-cooked egg yolks, mashed to a paste
2¼ cups all-purpose flour (do not use instant type)

½ teaspoon salt
Tiny red cinnamon drops and small pieces of angelica, green citron or candied cherries
1 egg white
1 tablespoon water
Red or green granulated sugar (optional)

Cream butter and confectioners' sugar, using electric mixer, if possible. Add lemon rind, rum and egg yolks. Mix well. Mix flour and salt. Add to first mixture and blend with hands. Chill dough until firm enough to handle. Break off one small piece at a time (a heaping teaspoonful) and roll into a pencil about 6 inches long. Shape in a circle; put circles 2 inches apart on cookie sheets. Pinch ends together and press 2 or 3 small red cinnamon drops into the dough at the joining to form a cluster of holly berries. Make tiny diamond-shape pieces of angelica or citron and press around the candies to represent leaves. Brush cookies with egg white slightly beaten with the water. You can also sprinkle the glazed surface with red or green sugar, which is often sold in shakers at Christmastime. Bake cookies in moderate oven (375°F.) until done, 8 to 10 minutes. Remove from oven at once, loosen cookies and cool. Makes about 5 dozen.

Chocolate Cookies

COCOA LOGS

(shown on plates 4 and 5)

Quick, not-too-sweet cookies.

½ cup butter or
  margarine, softened
6 tablespoons sugar,
  divided
2 tablespoons cocoa
1 teaspoon vanilla

⅛ teaspoon salt
1¼ cups flour
1 egg or egg white,
  slightly beaten
¼ cup finely chopped
  nuts

Cream butter, 4 tablespoons sugar, the cocoa, vanilla and salt until fluffy. Gradually stir in flour until blended. Divide dough in quarters. With lightly floured hands roll each in 18-inch rope. Place ropes parallel to each other and cut crosswise in 2-inch pieces. Brush with egg, then press tops in mixture of nuts and remaining 2 tablespoons sugar. Place 1 inch apart on lightly greased cookie sheet. Bake in preheated 350°F. oven 15 minutes or until firm to the touch. Remove to rack to cool. Makes 36.

CHOCOLATE NUT CRACKLES

Balls of dough are rolled in nuts, sugar and cinnamon before baking.

½ cup soft butter
1 cup light-brown
  sugar, packed
1 egg
1 square (1 ounce)
  unsweetened
  chocolate, melted
1¼ cups sifted flour
1 teaspoon cream of
  tartar

½ teaspoon baking
  soda
½ teaspoon salt
½ cup chopped
  toasted filberts or
  other nuts
2 tablespoons
  granulated sugar
2 teaspoons
  cinnamon

Cream butter, brown sugar and egg until light. Beat in cooled chocolate. Add sifted flour, cream of tartar, baking soda and salt; mix well. Chill. Then roll dough in 1-inch balls. Mix nuts, granulated sugar and cinnamon. Roll balls in the mixture and put on lightly greased cookie sheets. Bake in moderate oven (375°F.) 12 to 15 minutes. Makes about 3 dozen.

MOCHA NUT BUTTERBALLS

An old favorite with new mocha flavor.

1 cup soft butter
½ cup granulated
  sugar
2 teaspoons vanilla
2 teaspoons instant
  coffee powder
¼ cup cocoa

1¾ cups sifted flour
½ teaspoon salt
2 cups finely chopped
  pecans or
  California walnuts
Confectioners' sugar

Cream butter, sugar and vanilla until light. Add next 4 ingredients and mix well. Add nuts. Shape in 1-inch balls and put on cookie sheets. Bake in moderate oven (325°F.) about 15 minutes. Cool and roll in confectioners' sugar. Makes about 6 dozen.

TOASTED-ALMOND FINGERS

A delicious cookie dipped in chocolate.

1 cup butter or
  margarine, softened
½ cup confectioners'
  sugar
1 egg
1 teaspoon vanilla
2 cups sifted all-
  purpose flour
¼ teaspoon salt
1 cup toasted
  almonds, finely
  chopped

1 package (6 ounces)
  semisweet
  chocolate pieces
1 tablespoon
  vegetable
  shortening
Additional toasted
  almonds, finely
  chopped (optional)

Cream butter and sugar until fluffy. Add egg and beat well. Stir in vanilla. Add flour, salt and almonds and mix well. Wrap in waxed paper and chill until hard—about 30 minutes in freezer or several hours in refrigerator. Using measuring tablespoonfuls of dough, shape in 2-inch fingers and put on cookie sheet. Bake in slow oven (325°F.) 17 minutes, or until done. Cool on cake rack. Melt chocolate and shortening over hot water. Carefully dip one end of each finger in chocolate and put on waxed paper to dry. Sprinkle with nuts, if desired. Store in cool, dry place. Makes about 48.

CRISP CHOCOLATE-CHIP COOKIES

2 cups flour
1 teaspoon each
  baking soda and
  salt
1 cup butter or
  margarine, softened
1 cup packed brown
  sugar

½ cup granulated
  sugar
1 egg
1 teaspoon vanilla
1 package (12 ounces)
  semisweet
  chocolate pieces
1 cup chopped nuts

Mix flour, baking soda and salt; set aside. In large bowl of mixer cream butter and sugars until light. Beat in egg and vanilla until light and fluffy. With spoon stir in flour mixture, chocolate and nuts. Shape in 1-inch balls and place about 2 inches apart on cookie sheets. Bake in preheated 350°F. oven 15 minutes or until flat and browned. (Cookies will have soft centers.) Cool completely on cookie sheets. Store in airtight container. Makes about 54.

CHOCOLATE RINGS OR PRETZELS

Roll them in chopped nuts while they're hot.

½ cup margarine
⅔ cup sugar
1 egg, beaten
2 squares (2 ounces)
  unsweetened
  chocolate, melted

1 teaspoon vanilla
1½ cups sifted flour
1 teaspoon cinnamon
Chopped nuts

Cream together margarine and sugar. Beat in egg, then chocolate and vanilla. Add flour and cinnamon and blend thoroughly. Chill dough. Roll small pieces of dough between hands to thickness of a pencil. Shape into rings or pretzels. Bake on ungreased cookie sheet in moderate oven (350°F.) about 10 minutes. Roll cookies in chopped nut meats while they are hot. Makes 30 to 40 rings.

CHOCOLATE-FILLED AND COATED MACAROONS

More time-consuming than most, but worth the effort.

2 egg whites
¾ cup sugar
1¼ teaspoons vanilla, divided
1 cup blanched almonds, ground or chopped fine in blender or food processor (makes about 1¼ cups)
¼ cup fine dry bread crumbs
1 cup milk-chocolate pieces
1 square (1 ounce) unsweetened chocolate
3 tablespoons butter or margarine
1 egg, beaten
4 squares (4 ounces) semisweet chocolate, melted
Toasted chopped almonds

In bowl with whisk beat egg whites slightly (until foamy). Fold in sugar, ¼ teaspoon vanilla, the ground almonds and bread crumbs. Chill ½ hour. Using rounded measuring teaspoonfuls, shape dough in balls. (If sticky, rinse hands in cold water). Place balls 1 inch apart on well-greased floured cookie sheet. Bake in preheated 300°F. oven 18 to 20 minutes or until golden on bottom but still slightly moist (*do not overbake*). Cool 2 minutes; remove to rack to cool completely. In top of double boiler over simmering water melt milk chocolate, unsweetened chocolate and butter *without stirring*. Remove from water; beat until smooth. Beat in egg and remaining 1 teaspoon vanilla until smooth and shiny. Chill until stiff enough to spread, about 15 minutes. Mound measuring teaspoonful chocolate mixture on flat side of each macaroon, smoothing with small spatula. Chill 15 minutes. With small spatula quickly spread melted semisweet chocolate over chocolate-topped macaroons. Garnish with chopped almonds before glaze hardens. Store airtight in cool place. Makes 36.

GREEK CHOCOLATE BALLS

½ pound walnut meats
½ pound sweet cooking chocolate
9 pieces zwieback
½ teaspoon cinnamon
Confectioners' sugar
2 tablespoons rose water

Put nuts, chocolate and zwieback through food chopper, using fine blade. Add cinnamon, 1½ tablespoons sugar and rose water. Form into 36 small balls. Roll in confectioners' sugar. Store balls airtight. Can be frozen. Makes 36.

Jam-Filled Cookies

THIMBLE COOKIES

Rich short cookies topped with jam.

1 cup butter or margarine, softened	4 egg yolks
½ cup granulated or confectioners' sugar	1 teaspoon vanilla
	2 cups all-purpose flour
	Jam or jelly

Cream butter and sugar. Add egg yolks and vanilla and beat until light and fluffy. Stir in flour and, if necessary, chill until firm enough to handle. With floured hands, roll in 1-inch balls. Put 1½ inches apart on cookie sheets. Using a lightly floured thimble, make a small indentation in center of each cookie. Fill with jam. Bake in preheated 325°F. oven about 25 minutes. Cool on racks. Makes about 4 dozen.

FINGERPRINT COOKIES

2 cups flour	1 cup butter or margarine, softened
¾ cup confectioners' sugar	1 teaspoon vanilla
1 cup finely chopped nuts	Red-currant jelly

In mixing bowl combine flour, sugar and ½ cup nuts. With fork cut in butter until well distributed with dry ingredients. Sprinkle with vanilla and mix dough with hands until smooth. Shape in 1-inch balls, then roll in remaining ½ cup nuts, lightly pressing in nuts. Place about 1 inch apart on greased cookie sheets. Indent centers with lightly floured finger, then fill each with about ¼ teaspoon jelly. Bake in preheated 325°F. oven 15 to 18 minutes or until golden brown. Remove to rack to cool. Makes about 60.

ITALIAN NUT BALLS

Apricot jam and pistachio nuts give a distinctive flavor, but use walnuts if more convenient.

½ cup soft butter
⅓ cup sugar
1 egg, separated
¼ teaspoon each
   vanilla and almond
   extracts

1 cup sifted flour
½ teaspoon salt
¾ cup chopped
   pistachio nuts or
   colored walnuts
   (see below)
½ cup apricot jam

Cream butter; beat in sugar, egg yolk and flavorings. Add flour sifted with salt. Form into 36 small balls, using about ½ tablespoon of dough for each. Dip in slightly beaten egg white; then roll lightly in nuts. Put on buttered cookie sheets. With fingertip, make depression in center of each cookie. Bake in slow oven (300°F.) 25 minutes. While warm, fill centers with jam. Can be frozen. Makes 36.

Colored Walnuts. Add green food coloring to 2 teaspoons warm water; add ¾ cup chopped walnuts and blend thoroughly. Dry by placing on cookie sheet in moderate oven (350°F.) 8 minutes.

HUSSAR KISSES

A famous Austrian-Hungarian cookie with a dollop of jam on top.

⅔ cup sweet butter
   (must be butter and
   sweet is the best)
⅓ cup sugar
1 egg yolk

2 eggs
1⅓ cups sifted flour
⅓ cup finely chopped
   nuts
½ cup raspberry jam

Cream butter with sugar. Add egg yolk and 1 egg. Blend in flour. Chill. Pinch off walnut-size pieces of dough and shape into balls with floured hands. Put on ungreased cookie sheet. With pencil or finger make a deep depression in center of each ball. Beat remaining egg and brush cookies with it. Sprinkle with nuts. Bake in 350°F. oven 15 minutes, or until golden. Cool. Fill depression with jam. Makes about 32.

LINZER COOKIES

These outstanding cookies are Austrian in origin and make magnificent gifts.

½ cup softened (not runny or whipped) butter
½ cup sugar
1 egg yolk
Grated rind of ½ lemon
1 tablespoon lemon juice
1 tablespoon cocoa or grated unsweetened chocolate
1 cup all-purpose flour (instant type can be used)
½ cup each filberts and blanched almonds, finely ground, grated or whirled in blender
½ teaspoon cinnamon
½ teaspoon ground cloves
Red-raspberry jam
1 egg white mixed with
1 tablespoon water

Cream butter and sugar, using electric mixer, if available. Add egg yolk and beat until light and fluffy. Add grated rind and juice, then add cocoa and blend. Set aside. Mix flour, nuts and spices. Pour the butter-sugar-egg mixture into the dry ingredients, then mix with fork or hands as for piecrust. Dough will be on the soft side. Place in a bowl, cover and refrigerate 1 hour. Cookies can be shaped in several ways. The easiest is to take measuring half-teaspoonfuls of dough and roll into balls between floured palms. Place 1 inch apart on an ungreased sheet and with the little finger make an indentation in the center of each; do not punch through to the pan. Fill with a dab of red-raspberry jam. Another way is to put teaspoonfuls of dough into any individual tartlet or muffin pan, pressing dough into the bottom and sides to thickness of at least ⅓ inch, and add a dab of jam. If you wish, you can roll a small amount of dough about ¼ inch thick, and cut out strips with a fluted pie wheel or a dull knife, making them about ⅓ inch wide and the diameter of the tartlet pan. Cross two such strips over the top of each jam-filled tartlet. (Never fill more than two-thirds full.) Yet another way is to roll small amounts of dough at a time between floured pieces of waxed paper. Lift up the top piece and cut out dough with a 1½-inch round or fluted cookie cutter. Transfer to a cookie sheet, 1 inch apart. Brush with the egg white and water. Cut another batch of cookies, and with a thimble or tiny vegetable cutter, cut out the centers. Place the cookie rings over the solid circles. Press the edges together with the tines of a fork. Then put a half-teaspoonful of stiff jam in the center.

Brush the tops of the cookies or the strips of the tartlets with the egg white and water. Bake small cookies about 12 minutes and tartlets 18 to 20 minutes in moderate oven (375°F.). Loosen cookies when first removed from oven, but leave on pans until cooled. Loosen tartlets around edges when removing from oven and let remain in pans until cool. Then turn pans upside down and tap bottoms with the handle of a metal spoon or knife. Makes about 8 dozen small cookies or 4 dozen tartlets.

JAM DIAGONALS
(shown on plate 4)

Quick sliced cookies filled with jam and topped with lemon frosting.

½ cup butter or margarine, softened
¼ cup granulated sugar
1 teaspoon vanilla
⅛ teaspoon salt
1¼ cups flour
¼ cup seedless raspberry jam
¾ cup confectioners' sugar
4 teaspoons lemon juice

Cream butter, granulated sugar, vanilla and salt until fluffy. Gradually stir in flour until blended. Divide dough in thirds. On lightly floured surface with hands roll each in 9-inch rope. Place 3 inches apart on lightly greased cookie sheet. With finger make ½-inch depression down center of each rope (ropes will flatten to about 1-inch-wide strips). Fill depressions with jam. Bake in preheated 350°F. oven 12 to 15 minutes or until golden. Cool on cookie sheet. Blend confectioners' sugar and lemon juice until smooth; drizzle over jam. When icing is set, cut diagonally in 1-inch cookies. Makes about 24.

Nut Cookies

VANILLA FINGERS

Almonds and pistachio nuts make an appealing combination.

2½ cups all-purpose
flour
½ cup granulated
sugar (divided)
¼ teaspoon salt
½ cup minced
blanched almonds

1 cup butter or
margarine
2 teaspoons vanilla
1 egg, well beaten
¼ cup finely chopped
pistachio nuts or
other nuts

Combine flour, ¼ cup sugar, salt and almonds in mixing bowl. Cut in butter until particles resemble small peas. Sprinkle with vanilla and gather mixture into ball. (Do not handle dough too much.) Wrap dough in waxed paper and chill. Divide dough in 10 equal pieces. On lightly floured board, shape in thin rolls about ½ inch in diameter. Place rolls parallel, close to each other, and cut crosswise in 2-inch pieces. Brush one section at a time with egg, lift up one row with spatula and press surface into mixture of chopped nuts and remaining sugar. Put on ungreased baking sheets and bake in preheated 325°F. oven 20 minutes, or until light brown. Remove to rack to cool. Store airtight in cool place. Can be frozen. Good keepers. Makes about 7 dozen.

BROWN-SUGAR NUT MOUNDS

Easy, good keepers and shippers.

1 cup soft butter or
margarine
1½ cups light-brown
sugar, packed
1 egg
4 cups sifted flour
½ teaspoon salt

½ teaspoon baking
soda
2 teaspoons
cinnamon
½ cup commercial
sour cream
Pecan halves

Cream butter and sugar until light. Beat in egg. Add sifted dry ingredients and sour cream; mix well. Shape in balls the size of a small walnut. Put on sheets and press a pecan in center of each. Bake in hot oven (400°F.) 10 to 12 minutes. Makes about 7 dozen.

ALMOND CRESCENTS

The kirsch lightens the dough and makes the cookies tender.

1 cup sweet butter or margarine, softened
½ cup superfine granulated sugar, divided
5 tablespoons Vanilla Sugar, divided (recipe follows)

1 tablespoon kirsch or white rum
2 cups flour, divided
⅛ teaspoon salt
¾ cup blanched almonds, ground

In large bowl cream butter. Add 3 tablespoons superfine granulated sugar and 1 tablespoon Vanilla Sugar; beat until light and fluffy. Blend in kirsch. Stir in 1 cup flour and the salt. Stir in almonds and remaining 1 cup flour. Chill overnight. Lightly dust board or flat surface with remaining 5 tablespoons superfine granulated sugar. Break off small pieces of dough and roll with hands into pencil thin strips. Cut in 3-inch lengths; turn ends to form crescents. Arrange 1 inch apart on lightly greased cookie sheets. Bake in preheated 350°F. oven 12 to 15 minutes or until light golden brown. (They should remain almost white.) Cool on cookie sheet, then carefully remove and roll in remaining 4 tablespoons Vanilla Sugar. Makes 60.

VANILLA SUGAR Bury vanilla bean in jar with 2 cups superfine granulated sugar. Let stand a few days before using.

VIENNESE CRESCENTS

The best of all nut cookies, truly superb.

Combine the following: 1 cup ground walnuts or pecans, 1 cup butter (must be butter), ¾ cup sugar, 2½ cups sifted flour, and 1½ teaspoons vanilla. Knead to a smooth dough and shape about 1 teaspoon of dough at a time into small crescents, about 1½ inches long. Bake on ungreased cookie sheets in moderate oven (350°F.) until slightly browned, about 15 to 17 minutes. Cool 1 minute. While still warm, roll cookies in Vanilla Sugar (see below). Cool completely, and roll again in Vanilla Sugar. Makes about 70.

VANILLA SUGAR: Cut 2 or 3 vanilla beans into inch-long pieces. Place in a jar with 1 pound sifted confectioners' sugar. Let stand 3 days. The longer the sugar stands, the more fragrant.

PECAN, BRAZIL-NUT OR HAZELNUT MACAROONS

2 egg whites
⅛ teaspoon salt
1 cup packed dark-
  brown sugar
1¼ cups packed light-
  brown sugar

2 cups coarsely
  chopped pecans,
  Brazil nuts or
  hazelnuts
1 teaspoon vanilla
Nuts for garnishing
(optional)

There are two methods of mixing these ingredients. For the first, beat egg whites and salt very stiff, using electric mixer, if available. Gradually add sugar, beating constantly. Fold in nuts. Add vanilla. Method number two is used in the South: Grind the nuts and sugar together, then fold the stiffly beaten egg whites and salt into this and add flavoring. This makes a stiffer dough. Whichever method you use to blend the ingredients, take one rounded teaspoonful of dough at a time and roll into a ball. If dough sticks to hands, flour palms and continue rolling. Place balls 3 inches apart on buttered cookie sheet; they spread during baking. Flatten with the bottom of a tumbler or goblet dipped in flour. Do not flatten too thin; cookies should be about ½ inch thick. Half a pecan or hazelnut or a section of a Brazil nut can be pressed into the tops of macaroons before baking. Bake in moderate oven (350°F.) 10 to 12 minutes. Makes about 6 dozen.

WALNUT CRESCENTS
(shown on plate 4)

Hand-shaped cookies rich with nuts; good with fruit or ice cream.

½ cup butter or
  margarine, softened
¼ cup granulated
  sugar
1 teaspoon vanilla

⅛ inch teaspoon salt
⅓ cup finely chopped
  walnuts
1¼ cups flour
Confectioners' sugar

Cream butter, granulated sugar, vanilla and salt until fluffy. Stir in nuts. Gradually stir in flour until blended. Wrap airtight and chill 1 hour or longer. Pinch off walnut-size pieces. Roll in 4-inch fingers, tapering ends. Shape in crescents and place 1 inch apart on ungreased cookie sheet. Bake in preheated 350° F. oven 12 to 14 minutes or until golden. Remove to rack to cool. Sprinkle with confectioners' sugar sifted through small strainer. Makes about 18.

COFFEE-PECAN FANCIES

A perfect combination of delicious flavors.

½ cup margarine
½ cup granulated
  sugar
½ cup light-brown
  sugar, packed

½ teaspoon vanilla
2 tablespoons instant
  coffee
1 egg

1 cup sifted flour
¼ teaspoon salt
½ cup finely chopped
  pecans

Cream margarine; gradually beat in sugars, vanilla, coffee, and egg. Sift flour with salt; add to margarine mixture along with pecans. Chill. Form into marble-size balls; put on cookie sheets. Bake in moderate oven (350°F.) 10 minutes, or until lightly browned. Store in airtight container. Can be frozen. Makes 60.

FILBERT LEMON LOGS

The filberts are toasted for more delicious flavor.

1 cup butter or
  margarine
¾ cup light-brown
  sugar, packed

1 teaspoon grated
  lemon rind
2½ cups sifted flour
¼ teaspoon salt

1 tablespoon lemon
  juice
1 cup chopped,
  toasted filberts

Cream butter and sugar until light. Add lemon rind, sifted dry ingredients and lemon juice. Mix well and chill several hours. Shape in fingers. Roll in nuts and put on cookie sheets. Bake in hot oven (400°F.) 10 to 12 minutes. Makes 3 to 4 dozen.

SWEDISH FILBERT-BRANDY CRESCENTS
(Hasselnöt-Konjak-Halvmånar)

1 cup butter or
  margarine
Confectioners' sugar
1 tablespoon brandy
2 teaspoons water

1 cup chopped
  filberts
2 cups all-purpose
  flour (instant type
  can be used)

Cream butter and gradually add ½ cup sugar, creaming until light. Add brandy to the water and combine with creamed mixture. Add filberts and flour. Chill. Shape small pieces of dough into crescent shapes with hands and put on ungreased cookie sheet. Bake in a moderate oven (350°F.) 12 to 15 minutes. While still warm, roll in confectioners' sugar. Makes about 4 dozen crescents.

CHINESE ALMOND COOKIES

Brushing with egg gives a shiny top.

2 eggs
¾ cup sugar
⅔ cup vegetable oil
1 tablespoon orange
  juice
2 teaspoons almond
  extract
1 teaspoon vanilla

2½ cups sifted flour
1 teaspoon baking
  powder
¼ teaspoon salt
1 tablespoon water
⅓ cup blanched
  almonds

Beat 1 egg well; gradually add sugar and continue beating. Combine oil, orange juice and extracts; beat into egg and sugar mixture. Sift dry ingredients. Beat half into egg mixture and fold in remainder. Knead slightly until dough is smooth. Form into 1-inch balls and put on greased baking sheet. Flatten with fork or fingers. Slightly beat remaining egg with water; brush on cookies. Put almond in center. Bake in 350°F. oven 12 to 15 minutes. Makes 36.

SERINA CAKES

Chewy, rather sweet almond cookies of Norwegian derivation.

3¼ cups all-purpose
  flour
2 cups sugar, divided
1½ teaspoons baking
  powder
1¼ cups cold butter

2 eggs, separated
  (whites separated
  also)
1 teaspoon vanilla
1½ cups finely
  chopped blanched
  almonds

Combine flour, 1¾ cups sugar and the baking powder. Cut in butter until size of peas. Beat 1 egg white until stiff; gradually add remaining sugar, beating until stiff and shiny. Combine egg yolks and vanilla and fold into beaten white. Stir in flour mixture, then work well with fingertips until evenly distributed. Shape dough in 1-inch balls, brush with remaining egg white, slightly beaten, then roll in almonds. Put on well-greased cookie sheets, leaving space for cookies to spread. Flatten each slightly with fork or spatula. Bake in preheated 350°F. oven 15 minutes, or until golden brown. Cool slightly before removing to racks. Makes about 7½ dozen.

ALMOND TARTS
(shown on plates 4 and 5)

Bake ahead and freeze; serve unfilled or, for a quick dessert, fill with whipped cream and berries or a dab of jam.

½ cup butter or
    margarine, softened
¼ cup sugar
¼ teaspoon almond
    extract
⅛ teaspoon salt

1 egg white
½ cup blanched
    almonds, ground or
    grated
1¼ cups flour

In large bowl of mixer cream butter, sugar, almond extract and salt until fluffy. Add egg white and beat well. Stir in almonds and flour until blended. Wrap airtight and chill 1 hour or longer. Pinch off tablespoonfuls of dough and place in assorted fluted cookie molds (about 3½- or 2½-inch size). With lightly floured thumb press dough against bottom and sides, forming shell about ⅛ inch thick. Place molds on cookie sheet and bake in preheated 350°F. oven 10 to 12 minutes or until golden. While still slightly warm, turn molds upside down on cookie sheet and tap gently with spoon to loosen shells. Cool completely on rack. Makes about 24. **NOTE:** Fluted cookie molds are available in utensil specialty shops and in many houseware departments of large stores.

PEANUT CRESCENTS

¾ cup plus 2
    tablespoons
    margarine
¼ cup granulated
    sugar
2 cups all-purpose
    flour

1 teaspoon vanilla
½ cup coarsely
    crushed salted
    peanuts (see Note)
Confectioners' sugar

Cream butter and granulated sugar well. Add flour and 1 tablespoon water and mix well, then add vanilla and peanuts. Wrap in waxed paper or plastic and store in refrigerator overnight. Next day, shape mixture in crescents, using about 1 teaspoonful dough for each. Put on ungreased sheets and bake in moderate oven (350°F.) about 15 minutes. Roll in confectioners' sugar while warm. Makes about 6 dozen. **NOTE:** Crush peanuts on board with rolling pin. Do not whirl in blender. Use unsalted peanuts if desired.

GREEK ALMOND COOKIES
(Kourabiedes)

A traditional Greek Christmas cookie. Each almond-shaped cookie is studded with a whole clove, a reminder of the aromatic gifts brought by the Magi to the Christ Child.

2 cups flour
½ teaspoon baking powder
1 cup butter or margarine, softened
¼ cup plus 2 tablespoons confectioners' sugar, divided

1 egg yolk
2 tablespoons brandy
½ teaspoon vanilla
½ cup finely chopped blanched almonds
36 whole cloves

Stir together flour and baking powder; set aside. In large bowl cream butter. Gradually add ¼ cup confectioners' sugar; beat until fluffy. Add egg yolk, brandy and vanilla; beat until very light. Stir in almonds. By hand stir in flour mixture to form soft, smooth dough. Chill 30 minutes or until easy to handle. Shape level tablespoonfuls of dough into ovals (almond shape and size). Place 1 inch apart on ungreased baking sheets. Press whole clove in center of each. Bake in preheated 325°F. oven 25 to 30 minutes or until sand color, not brown. Remove to racks to cool. Before serving, dust generously with remaining 2 tablespoons confectioners' sugar. Makes 36.

Fruit Cookies

OATMEAL-RAISIN COOKIES

Crunchy, chewy little hand-shaped balls, good with milk.

½ cup butter or
   margarine, softened
¾ cup packed brown
   sugar
1 teaspoon vanilla
⅛ teaspoon salt

½ cup raisins
1¼ cups rolled oats
¾ cup flour
¾ teaspoon baking
   soda

Cream butter, sugar, vanilla and salt until fluffy. Stir in raisins and oats until well blended. Stir together flour and baking soda; gradually stir into creamed mixture until blended. Shape in 1-inch balls and place 1½ inches apart on lightly greased cookie sheet. Bake in preheated 375°F. oven 13 to 15 minutes or until light brown. Cool 5 minutes. Remove to rack to cool completely. Makes about 36.

DATE-RAISIN-NUT COOKIES

A hint of brandy or bourbon gives these a subtle flavor.

1 cup flour
1 teaspoon baking
   powder
¼ teaspoon salt
½ cup butter or
   margarine, softened
1 cup nuts, chopped
   fine

1 cup flaked
   sweetened or
   unsweetened
   coconut
½ cup packed finely
   cut-up pitted dates
½ cup raisins
1 egg
2 teaspoons brandy or
   bourbon

In bowl mix flour, baking powder and salt. Cut in butter until particles are size of peas. Stir in nuts, coconut, dates, raisins, egg and brandy. Mix with wooden spoon or hand until dough forms. Chill 1 hour. Shape in 1-inch balls. Place ½ inch apart on greased cookie sheet. With tines of fork dipped in flour, flatten balls to form 1½-inch cookies. Bake in preheated 350°F. oven 15 minutes or until golden brown. Makes 48.

CEREAL-DATE WREATHS

(shown on plate 4)

Hand-shaped orange-flavored cookies rolled in crushed cereal.

½ cup butter or margarine, softened
¼ cup sugar
1 teaspoon vanilla
⅛ teaspoon salt
1 egg
Grated peel of 1 orange or 1 lemon
½ cup finely chopped dates
1¼ cups flour
1 cup whole wheat flakes or corn flakes, crushed fine

In large bowl of mixer cream butter, sugar, vanilla and salt until fluffy. Add egg and beat well. Stir in orange peel and dates. Gradually stir in flour until blended. Wrap dough airtight and chill 1 hour or longer. Pinch off walnut-size pieces of dough. Roll each piece in cereal (on flat surface) to 4½-inch-long rope. Shape in wreaths, pinching ends together. Place 1 inch apart on lightly greased cookie sheet. Bake in preheated 350°F. oven 12 to 14 minutes or until light brown. Remove to rack to cool. Makes about 24.

RAISIN PFEFFERNEUSSE

A version of the classic Christmas pepper cookie, chock full of raisins.

1 box (15 ounces) raisins
1 cup almonds
¼ cup cut-up citron
2 cups flour
2 teaspoons cinnamon
1 teaspoon cloves
½ teaspoon each baking powder, baking soda, salt and freshly ground pepper
3 eggs
2 cups packed light-brown sugar
Confectioners' sugar

With fine blade of food grinder, grind raisins, almonds and citron into bowl; set aside. Stir together flour, cinnamon, cloves, baking powder, baking soda, salt and pepper and mix into raisin mixture. In large bowl of electric mixer beat eggs and sugar until fluffy; stir into raisin-flour mixture and mix well with large spoon (dough will be stiff). Chill about 1 hour. With floured hands form 1-inch balls and place 2 inches apart on well-greased baking sheet. Bake in preheated 350°F. oven 10 minutes, or until cookies are brown on bottom but still soft on top. Remove to rack. While still warm, shake in bag with confectioners' sugar; cool. Store airtight at least 1 week before eating. Makes about 8 dozen.

CURRANT COOKIES

Lemon peel adds zest.

¾ cup currants
1 cup butter or
   margarine, softened
¼ cup sugar

Grated peel of 1
  lemon
2¼ cups flour

Plump currants in hot water to cover 5 minutes; drain well; set aside. Cream butter and sugar until fluffy. Stir in currants and lemon peel. Gradually stir in flour, then mix dough with hands until smooth. Shape in 1-inch balls and place about 1 inch apart on greased cookie sheets. Dip tines of fork in flour and flatten balls to about 1½-inch cookies. Bake in preheated 350°F. oven 10 to 12 minutes or until golden. Remove to rack to cool. Makes about 66.

ROOKIE'S *HAMANTASCHEN*

A three-cornered prune-filled pastry traditionally served for Purim, a joyous Jewish festival celebrated in early spring.

2½ cups flour
2 tablespoons sugar
1½ teaspoons baking
  powder
¼ teaspoon salt
⅔ cup margarine

1 egg
⅓ cup orange juice
¼ cup sugar mixed
  with ½ teaspoon
  cinnamon
Prune-Nut Filling
  (recipe follows)

In bowl combine flour, sugar, baking powder and salt. With pastry blender or 2 knives cut in margarine until mixture resembles coarse crumbs. Stir in egg and orange juice; mix just to combine. Gather in ball, wrap and chill. Divide dough in half. On floured pastry cloth or other surface roll out each half ¹⁄₁₆ inch thick to about 14-inch circle. Using 10-ounce custard cup or 4½-inch cutter, cut out 10 circles. Sprinkle both sides lightly with sugar-cinnamon mixture. Place rounded tablespoon of filling on center of each circle. Lift edges of dough around filling, leaving center open, and pinch edges together firmly, forming three-cornered pastry. Using wide spatula, place pastries about 2 inches apart on ungreased cookie sheets. Bake in preheated 350°F. oven 20 minutes or until light golden brown. Cool on racks. Makes 20.

PRUNE-NUT FILLING In saucepan bring to boil 1 can (12 ounces) pitted prunes and ½ cup water. Cover, then simmer until prunes are very soft and lose their shape, 10 to 15 minutes. Remove from heat. With potato masher or fork mash prunes well. Stir in ½ cup sugar, ½ cup chopped walnuts and 1 teaspoon cinnamon; mix well. Makes about 1¾ cups.

WHITE COCONUT COOKIES

An ever-so-thin, almost lacy coconut flake.

1 cup butter, softened	6 tablespoons water
Sugar	2 cups all-purpose
1 cup flaked coconut	flour

Cream butter and 1¾ cups sugar. Add remaining ingredients and mix well. Chill 30 minutes, or until firm enough to handle, then roll in walnut-size balls, flouring hands if necessary. Put on greased cookie sheets and press thin with bottom of glass tumbler, buttered and dipped in sugar. Bake in moderate oven (375°F.) 10 minutes, or until browned and crisp. Let stand a few minutes before removing to racks. Makes about 5 dozen. Stored airtight, cookies keep 1 week at room temperature or in refrigerator, 3 weeks in freezer.

TOASTED-ALMOND COOKIES Use above recipe, substituting 1 cup toasted chopped blanched almond slivers for the coconut. Sprinkle unbaked cookies with colored sugar. Makes about 4 dozen. Stored airtight, cookies keep about a week at room temperature, 2 weeks in refrigerator or 3 weeks in freezer.

COCONUT DIAMONDS

These can be made with standard kitchen tools, but they are easy in a food processor.

1⅓ cups moist flaked coconut	½ teaspoon salt
1 cup butter or margarine, softened	½ teaspoon vanilla
1 cup sugar	2¾ cups flour
	Rum Icing (recipe follows)

Whirl coconut in blender until finely grated; set aside. Cream butter, sugar, salt and vanilla until fluffy. Stir in coconut and flour. Gather in ball. (In food processor, using steel blade, whirl coconut until finely grated. Add remaining ingredients except icing; whirl to form dough.) Cut in 9 portions. Shape each in rope ¾ inch thick. With fingers press each rope out on cookie sheet lined with waxed paper to form 12 × 1½-inch strip (3 to a cookie sheet, 3 inches apart). Bake in preheated 375°F. oven until edges are browned, 8 to 10 minutes. With flexible spatula loosen cookie strips from paper but leave on sheet. While warm, gently spread with icing, then slice diagonally in ¾-inch pieces. Remove to racks to cool. Makes about 108.

RUM ICING Mix 2½ cups confectioners' sugar and enough dark Jamaica rum (5 to 6 tablespoons) to make a thin icing.

FIG GRAHAM COOKIES

1 cup margarine,
  softened
1½ cups sugar
2 eggs
Grated rind of 1
  lemon
2 cups unsifted all-
  purpose flour
1½ cups whole-wheat
  flour

1½ teaspoons cream
  of tartar
1½ teaspoons baking
  soda
½ teaspoon salt
16 (about 12 ounces)
  golden dried figs,
  chopped (2 cups)

Cream margarine and sugar. Add eggs and lemon rind and beat until fluffy. Stir in remaining ingredients. Shape mixture in 1-inch mounds on cookie sheets and flatten by pressing crisscross with floured tines of fork. Bake in preheated 400°F. oven 8 to 10 minutes. Makes 84. **NOTE:** Recipe can be halved.

ORANGE-GINGER COOKIES

⅔ cup shortening,
  melted
Sugar
¼ cup molasses
1 egg
⅓ cup each finely
  diced candied
  orange peel,
  crystallized ginger
  and chopped
  toasted almonds

2½ cups flour
1 teaspoon baking
  soda
¼ teaspoon salt
1 teaspoon ginger
½ teaspoon cloves
Slivered almonds

Pour shortening into mixing bowl and cool. Add 1 cup sugar, the molasses and egg and mix well with wooden spoon; stir in orange peel, crystallized ginger and chopped nuts. Stir together flour, baking soda, salt, ginger and cloves; add ¼ at a time to sugar mixture, mixing well with hands. With lightly floured hands shape in 1-inch balls, roll in sugar and place on lightly greased cookie sheets 1½ inches apart. Flatten slightly with spatula and press slivered almond in center of each. Bake in preheated 325°F. oven 12 to 15 minutes (do not overbake; cookies should be chewy). Cool on rack. Makes about 7 dozen.

Spice Cookies

MOLASSES CRINKLES

The water makes them crinkle.

¾ cup soft butter
1 cup light-brown
sugar, packed
1 egg
¼ cup molasses
2¼ cups sifted flour

2 teaspoons baking
soda
1 teaspoon cinnamon
1 teaspoon ginger
½ teaspoon cloves
¼ teaspoon salt
Granulated sugar

Cream butter, brown sugar, egg, and molasses until light. Add sifted dry ingredients and mix well. Chill. Roll in 1-inch balls and dip in granulated sugar. Put 3 inches apart on lightly greased cookie sheets. Sprinkle each cookie with 2 or 3 drops of water. Bake in moderate oven (375°F.) 8 to 10 minutes. Makes 48.

PEPPER-AND-SPICE COOKIES
(shown on plate 5)

Lightly spiced semicrisp balls with a hint of black-pepper flavor.

1½ cups flour
1 teaspoon baking
soda
½ teaspoon each
cinnamon, cloves
and ginger
⅛ teaspoon pepper
½ cup butter or
margarine, softened
⅓ cup packed brown
sugar

1 tablespoon dark
corn syrup
⅛ teaspoon salt
1 egg, separated
1 tablespoon milk
Pecan or walnut
halves or whole
blanched almonds

Stir together flour, baking soda, cinnamon, cloves, ginger and pepper; set aside. In large bowl of mixer cream butter, sugar, corn syrup and salt until fluffy. Add egg white and beat well. Gradually stir in flour mixture until blended. Wrap dough airtight and chill ½ hour. Shape in 1-inch balls and place 1 inch apart on lightly greased cookie sheet. Beat egg yolk with milk; brush on cookies and press a nut half in center of each. Brush again with egg mixture. Bake in preheated 350°F. oven 13 to 15 minutes or until light brown. Remove to rack to cool. Makes about 32.

NUTMEG LOGS

1 cup soft butter	1 egg
2 teaspoons vanilla	3 cups sifted flour
2 teaspoons rum	Nutmeg
flavoring	¼ teaspoon salt
¾ cup sugar	Frosting

Cream butter with flavorings; gradually beat in sugar. Blend in egg. Sift flour, 1 teaspoon nutmeg and salt; add to butter mixture and mix well. Shape pieces of dough on sugared board into long rolls ½ inch in diameter. Cut in 3-inch lengths and put on buttered cookie sheets. Bake in moderate oven (350°F.) 12 to 15 minutes. Cool. Spread frosting on top and sides of cookies; mark with tines of fork to resemble bark. Sprinkle lightly with nutmeg. Can be frozen. Makes 72.

FROSTING: Cream ⅓ cup butter with 1 teaspoon vanilla and 2 teaspoons rum flavoring. Blend in 2 cups sifted confectioners' sugar and 2 tablespoons light cream; beat until smooth and creamy.

MEXICAN SESAME ANISE COOKIES

Sesame and aniseed are a pleasing combination.

1 tablespoon aniseed	⅛ teaspoon baking
2 tablespoons boiling	soda
water	2 eggs
¾ cup butter	2 cups sifted flour
⅔ cut sugar	3 tablespoons sesame
	seed, toasted

Combine aniseed and boiling water and steep while mixing dough. Cream butter with sugar and baking soda. Beat in 1 egg. Drain aniseed and add. Stir in flour, a little at a time. Mix well. Chill dough overnight. Roll dough into ½-inch balls. Place on ungreased cookie sheets 1½ inches apart. Put a piece of waxed paper over cookies and flatten to ¹⁄₁₆-thickness with bottom of a glass. Remove waxed paper. Beat remaining egg and brush tops. Sprinkle with sesame seed. Bake in hot oven (400°F.) 7 or 8 minutes. Makes 12 dozen.

NOTE: To toast sesame seeds place in shallow pan in moderate oven (350°F.) 10 minutes, or until golden brown, stirring occasionally.

SWEDISH HORSESHOE COOKIES
(Hästskor)

Cardamon gives these a traditionally festive Scandinavian flavor.

1 cup butter or margarine	2 teaspoons cinnamon
¾ cup sugar	1 teaspoon baking soda
1½ tablespoons molasses	1 tablespoon water
8 cardamom seeds, crushed, or ½ teaspoon ground cardamom	2½ cups all-purpose flour (instant type can be used)
	1 egg white

Cream butter, add ¾ cup sugar and cream together thoroughly. Add molasses, cardamom and cinnamon. Dissolve baking soda in the water and add with the flour. Blend to a smooth dough. Chill. Roll out on floured board. Cut in strips 4 inches × ½ inch, and form into horseshoe shapes and press with floured fork. Brush tops with slightly beaten egg white and sprinkle with sugar. Bake in moderate oven (375°F.) about 8 minutes. Makes about 5 dozen.

GINGER CREAMS

½ cup butter or margarine, softened	1 tablespoon ginger
¾ cup sugar	1 teaspoon baking soda
1 egg	Filling
¼ cup molasses	Confectioners' sugar (optional)
2 cups all-purpose flour	

Cream butter and sugar until light and fluffy. Add egg and molasses and beat well. Stir in sifted flour, ginger and soda. Roll in small balls, put on greased cookie sheet and flatten with glass dipped in water. Bake in moderate oven (350°F.) 12 minutes, or until done. Sandwich with filling between, or serve plain. Sprinkle with confectioners' sugar, if desired. Makes 7 dozen plain cookies or 3½ dozen filled cookies.

FILLING

3 tablespoons butter or margarine, melted	2 cups confectioners' sugar
¾ teaspoon vanilla	3 tablespoons brandy

Combine all ingredients and mix until blended.

GINGER STICKS

3 eggs
½ pound light-brown
   sugar
3¼ cups sifted flour
½ teaspoon baking
   powder

½ teaspoon salt
1 teaspoon cinnamon
1 teaspoon ground
   cloves
¾ cup diced candied
   ginger

Beat eggs until thick and lemon-colored; gradually beat in sugar. Sift flour, baking powder, salt and spices; add to egg mixture with ginger. Chill 1 hour. Turn out on a sugared board and form into a roll 2 inches in diameter; cut in 2-inch lengths and roll each to a rope the size of a crayon. Cut in 1½-inch sticks and put on buttered cookie sheets. Bake in slow oven (300°F.) 8 to 10 minutes or until done. Store in airtight container. Can be frozen. Makes 144.

GERMAN PFEFFERNEUSSE

These holiday cookies are frosted before being stored to ripen.

3 cups sifted flour
¾ teaspoon each salt,
   baking powder,
   allspice, mace,
   cardamom
¼ teaspoon black
   pepper
¾ teaspoon baking
   soda

⅛ teaspoon ground
   aniseed
1 cup honey
3 tablespoons
   shortening
1 egg
Frosting

Sift dry ingredients. Heat honey (do not boil). Add shortening. Cool. Beat in egg. Stir in dry ingredients just until blended. Let dough stand 10 minutes to stiffen enough to handle easily. Shape in 1-inch balls. Place on lightly greased cookie sheets. Bake in moderate oven (350°F.) 13 to 15 minutes. Cool; frost. Store airtight a week to ripen. Makes 60.

FROSTING:Combine 1 egg white, 2 teaspoons honey and ¼ teaspoon ground aniseed. Gradually add 1½ cups sifted confectioners' sugar, beating until smooth. Put 12 to 14 cookies in a bowl, add 2 tablespoons frosting and stir to frost all sides of cookies. Lift out with a fork onto rack. Repeat until all are frosted.

NORWEGIAN "BROWN BREADS"
(Brun Brod)

*These are actually cookies flavored with cardamom and
topped with pearl sugar.*

1 cup butter or margarine, softened	½ teaspoon baking soda
1 cup packed brown sugar	1 cup finely chopped almonds
1 egg	2½ cups flour
1 teaspoon crushed cardamom	About ½ cup pearl sugar or coarsely crushed sugar cubes
1 teaspoon cinnamon	
1 teaspoon baking powder	

Cream butter and brown sugar until fluffy, then beat in egg. Stir in cardamom,
cinnamon, baking powder, baking soda and almonds. Stir in flour until well
blended and dough is stiff. Shape in ¾-inch balls. Dip tops in pearl sugar,
pressing it in slightly. Place balls sugar side up on lightly greased cookie sheets.
Bake in preheated 350°F. oven 8 to 10 minutes or until light golden. Remove to
racks to cool. Makes about 72.

GERMAN ANISE COOKIES

2 eggs	1 tablespoon hot water
1½ cups packed dark-brown sugar	2 cups flour
¼ teaspoon salt	1 tablespoon whole aniseed
½ teaspoon baking soda dissolved in	1 cup granulated sugar

In large bowl beat eggs at medium speed of electric mixer until very light.
Gradually beat in brown sugar (any soft lumps will blend in); continue beating
15 minutes. (Mixture should be very thick.) Stir in salt and dissolved baking
soda. Fold in flour and aniseed until well blended. Put granulated sugar in pie
plate. With lightly greased or oiled hands (dough will be sticky; do not add flour)
form dough in balls the size of hickory nuts (slightly less than ¾-inch diameter).
Roll in sugar to coat. Arrange 1½ inches apart on greased cookie sheets. Bake in
preheated 375°F. oven 8 to 10 minutes or until light brown. Cookies will puff up
during baking, then flatten and crackle on top when done. They are soft when
taken from oven, but quickly become firm. Makes 108. **NOTE:** Cookies become
crisp when stored; flavor improves with age.

VIII
PRESSED COOKIES

Decorated with colored sugar, pressed cookies are traditional favorites during the holidays, and for festive occasions the year round.

Pressed cookies are made by filling a cookie press with dough and pushing small shapes out with a plunger onto a cookie sheet. Presses come with interchangeable pattern disks.

The term "pressed cookies" also refers to another, somewhat related, shaping technique whereby a repeating design is impressed into a sheet of dough and baked. In this case, the "press" is a thin wooden slab, block or carved cylinder, handled like a rolling pin. The designs are sliced separate before baking.

Most of the flat presses are hand carved and imported from Middle European countries—Austria, Hungary and Czechoslovakia.

In either case, many dough recipes can be used to make pressed cookies. Test to see the dough is firm enough (but not stiff) to retain the press pattern while baking.

SPRITZ COOKIES

Crisp vanilla cookies.

1 cup butter or
  margarine, softened
¾ cup granulated
  sugar
1 egg
1 teaspoon vanilla

2¼ cups all-purpose
  flour
¼ teaspoon salt
Colored sugar
  (optional)

Cream butter, then gradually add granulated sugar, creaming well. Beat in egg and vanilla. Gradually stir in flour mixed with the salt. Press dough through cookie press in various shapes onto cold ungreased cookie sheets. Sprinkle with colored sugar, if desired. Bake in preheated 375°F. oven 10 minutes, or until edges are lightly browned. Cool on racks. Makes 7 to 8 dozen, depending on size.

BROWN-SUGAR SPRITZ

Another version of the popular Spritz. Pressed cookies are Scandinavian holiday favorites. These have a caramel flavor and are quick to make. Spritz cookie presses are available in Scandinavian gift or gourmet cookware shops.

1 cup butter or margarine, softened	¼ cup heavy cream
1 cup packed brown sugar	1 teaspoon vanilla
3 egg yolks	½ teaspoon baking powder
	3 cups flour

Cream butter and sugar until light. Beat in egg yolks and cream until smooth and fluffy. Stir in vanilla and baking powder. Stir in flour until blended. (If dough seems too soft, chill.) Put in cookie press and press out desired shapes (rings, bars, rosettes and *S*'s) on ungreased *cool* cookie sheets. Bake in preheated 375°F. oven 8 to 10 minutes or until cookies are light golden around edges. Remove to racks to cool. Makes about 96.

CHOCOLATE-ALMOND SPRITZ COOKIES

½ cup butter or margarine, softened	2 teaspoons milk
1 cup sugar	1 teaspoon vanilla
1 egg	1¼ cups flour
2 squares (2 ounces) unsweetened chocolate, melted and cooled	½ cup ground roasted almonds
	½ teaspoon salt
	Confectioners' sugar (optional)

Cream together butter and sugar until fluffy. Beat in egg until light and fluffy. Add chocolate, milk and vanilla. Blend well. Gradually stir in flour, almonds and salt until well blended. Chill at least 2 hours. Press through cookie press in desired shapes about 1 inch apart on ungreased cookie sheets. Bake in preheated 350°F. oven 8 to 10 minutes or until top springs back when pressed lightly with fingertips. Cool on cookie sheets 1 minute; remove to racks to cool completely. Sprinkle with confectioner's sugar. Store in airtight container in cool, dry place. Will keep about 2 weeks. Makes about 85.

APPENDIX:

Metric Conversion Tables

TEMPERATURES	POUNDS TO GRAMS

TEMPERATURES

Fahrenheit°
Celsius°
180°F/82°C
190°F/88°C
200°F/95°C
225°F/107°C
250°F/120°C
275°F/135°C
285°F/140°C
300°F/150°C
325°F/165°C
350°F/180°C
375°F/190°C
400°F/205°C
425°F/220°C
450°F/230°C
475°F/245°C
500°F/260°C
525°F/275°C
550°F/290°C

POUNDS TO GRAMS

Pounds	Convenient Equivalent
¼ lb	115 g
½ lb	225 g
¾ lb	340 g
1 lb	450 g

OUNCES TO GRAMS

Ounces	Convenient Equivalent
1 oz	30 g
2 oz	60 g
3 oz	85 g
4 oz	115 g
5 oz	140 g
6 oz	180 g
8 oz	225 g
9 oz	250 g
10 oz	285 g
12 oz	340 g
14 oz	400 g
16 oz	450 g
20 oz	560 g
24 oz	675 g

LIQUID MEASURE CONVERSIONS

Cups and Spoons	Liquid Ounces	Approximate Metric Term	Approximate Centiliters
1 tsp.	⅙ oz	1 tsp	½ cL
1 Tb	½ oz	1 Tb	1½ cL
¼ c; 4 Tb	2 oz	½ dL; 4 Tb	6 cL
⅓ c; 5 Tb	2⅔ oz	¾ dL; 5Tb	8 cL
½ c	4 oz	1 dL	12 cL
⅔ c	5⅓ oz	1½ dL	15 cL
¾ c	6 oz	1¾ dL	18 cL
1 c	8 oz	¼ L	24 cL

INCHES TO CENTIMETERS

Inches ("in")	Centimeters ("cm") (Nearest Equivalent)	Inches ("in")	Centimeters ("cm") (Nearest Equivalent)
1/16 in	¼ cm	3 in	8 cm
⅛ in	½ cm	3½ in	9 cm
3/16 in	"less than ¼ in/¾ cm"	4 in	10 cm
		5 in	13 cm
¼ in	¾ cm	6 in	15 cm
⅜ in	1 cm	7 in	18 cm
½ in	1½ cm	8 in	20 cm
⅝ in	1½ cm	9 in	23 cm
¾ in	2 cm	10 in	25 cm
1 in	2½ cm	12 in	30 cm
1½ in	4 cm	14 in	35 cm
2 in	5 cm	15 in	38½ cm
2½ in	6½ cm	16 in	40 cm

Index